THE CHOICE

THE
CHOICE

A Practical Guide on the Moral Issue

Larry W. Tippetts

**Foreword by
Brenton G. Yorgason**

Bookcraft
Salt Lake City, Utah

Library of Congress Catalog Card Number: 84-70068
ISBN 0-88494-521-9

First Printing, 1984

Lithographed in the United States of America
PUBLISHERS PRESS
Salt Lake City, Utah

Contents

Foreword

Recently I was flying over the vast desert terrain of Saudi Arabia. As I gazed from the window of the plane, I searched eagerly for something different, something that would tell me exactly how far I had yet to travel before reaching my destination. Even though the area consisted of rolling plains of sand, every few minutes I would see a small cluster of trees surrounded by nomadic tents. It soon became apparent that if I were creating a map from which to trace my steps, I would use these oases as landmarks to direct my course.

Returning now to the soil of the gospel, I find that its richness is amazingly surrounded by equally vast and arid plains of spiritual desert. Even though the surrounding world has largely become amoral as regards sexual intimacy, and has no concept of its sacredness, still we must live in this world and interact with those spiritual nomads who are wandering in search of even a small amount of nourishment.

As I consider the contents of this book, and the truly life-supporting food that it offers young Latter-day Saints, I must eagerly declare it to be a rare and precious landmark from which the youth can chart their spiritual course.

Almost two decades ago the author and I were tracting the streets of Jacksonville, Florida, as full-time missionaries. At that time we talked of our personal values, and there we inspired each other to live the higher moral law and so be guided in our selection of an eternal mate. Little did we know that, even at that same hour, our future companions were themselves serving as lady missionaries in other parts of the world, strengthening their own moral fiber so that they similarly would be worthy of their future husbands.

Since that rainy day in Florida, the author has become professionally involved in the lives of the youth, with the intent of doing his part to assist *them* through the spiritual desert of today's world.

These chapters, carefully and prayerfully brought together by the author, represent years of study and of interaction with youth. In this the author has been sensitive to their needs, their desires, and especially their feelings. In an exciting and straightforward way, these experiences have now been committed to paper. These pages will not only serve to assist parents and leaders but will be a true oasis from which the youth can safely quench their thirst as they begin to understand the powerful and sacred procreative process.

BRENTON G. YORGASON

Acknowledgments

The writing of this book was stimulated in part by an article written by Elder Neal A. Maxwell in the *New Era* (June 1979, pp. 36-43). In this article, "The Stern But Sweet Seventh Commandment," Elder Maxwell writes:

> It is important for you to be philosophical defenders as well as practicers of chastity. Articulate advocacy is surely needed now with regard to some of the damaging balderdash we see and hear in the world pertaining to immoral life-styles.
>
> Austin Farrer warned, "Though argument does not create conviction, the lack of [it] destroys belief. What seems to be proved may not be embraced; but what no one shows the ability to defend is quickly abandoned."

For the introduction of this crucial germ, I express appreciation. I wish also to thank the students and instructors of the Church Educational System for providing the motivation for me to share my written feelings on this sensitive topic. In addition, I would like to thank Brenton G. Yorgason for his timely encouragement and his foreword, Lenore Burkhardt and Norma Ericson for their assistance in typing various drafts of this book, and Max Caldwell and Lynn Scoresby for seminal ideas presented in their lectures.

1

Our Procreative Power

Trent* has a problem! His roommate introduced him to a great-looking girl a few weeks ago. Their immediate attraction for each other resulted in a daily lunch date at the cafeteria. Although they have yet to be on a formal date, and although they have exchanged no physical affection, Trent is in a quandary. You see, while they were walking together across campus a few days ago, she turned to Trent and said, "How would you feel if I suggested we go to bed together?" (That's a direct quote!)

The next day a visibly shaken Trent entered my office and related the experience to me. He was attending my Preparation for Marriage class at the institute, having recently returned from a full-time mission. Living in the dorms and not yet acquainted with his new bishop, he felt a need to confide in someone he knew. As I listened, Trent explained that he was having some feelings he had never before experienced. Never had a girl shown such obvious interest in him. He was definitely attracted to her, and until her suggestion of the day before he had thought she'd make a great Latter-day Saint. Although he turned down her proposal, she con-

---

*The experiences related throughout this book are true, but names and places have been changed.

1

tinued to act friendly and seemed interested in pursuing the relationship.

"I guess I'm wondering how strong I really am. I've never had this kind of challenge to my values. I still feel physically attracted to her despite the dangerous ground I'm walking on. I just can't get her out of my mind!"

Unusual situation? Not really. At least not for the Trents and Todds and Kathys and Sharons who are struggling to deal with the powerful (but normal) physical drives within them while living in a world where satisfying those desires *now* is the norm. The hormones, society's standards, the media, and the (so-called) experts all tend to move today's young person along a wide, broad path leading to physical gratification.

For a youth raised during the decades of the 70s and 80s, without the benefit of clearly defined standards, the result is almost inevitable. For a young Latter-day Saint, raised with daily reminders from prophets, parents, and scripture to *be clean,* the dilemma is more acute. Even when today's LDS youth is positive of the benefits of chastity, the world is ever with him, and given the right series of circumstances, many—far too many—fall prey to the sin that is next to murder in seriousness.

Latter-day Saints have the same glands and bodily functionings as their peers (who often have a more permissive attitude toward coping with those urges). In times of weakness or forgetfulness those physical desires tend to dominate, resulting in remorse and regret following the transgression. One young high school girl, feeling the reality of the above, asks, "Wouldn't it be much easier on everyone if the Lord had activated this power only after marriage?" Another young man wonders: "Why did God make me this way? If these things are so wrong, why does it seem so natural?"

Part of the confusion stems from false ideas that have been taught regarding man's basic nature. Many believe that man is only an advanced form of animal: he has no spirit, the body is the only reality, and life's purpose is to gratify the physical appetites. Many of the major world religions, including some branches of Christianity, teach that the body is evil and will be discarded permanently at death. Even as members of the Church of Jesus Christ we stumble at times over misunderstood passages, such as "the natural man is an enemy to God" (Mosiah 3:19); "men began . . . to be carnal, sensual, and devilish" (Moses 5:13); or "thy children are conceived in sin" (Moses 6:55).

In contrast, the truth of the matter, as taught in the scriptures and emphasized by living prophets, is that the body is a great blessing, and although the spirit must eventually learn to dominate the physical appetites, the body will never be discarded permanently. In fact, that lovable (sometimes overweight) few pounds of flesh that you and I received at birth was an anxiously awaited addition to our eternal personality. The body enables us to experience a fulness of joy in the creative process as parents, and adds a great deal to our enjoyment of mortal existence now. Consider those spirits who were cast out of heaven for rebellion, without opportunity to have physical bodies. They would do virtually anything to have one—even take the body of a swine rather than be left as spirits (see Matthew 8:28-32).

Because many people in the world lack an adequate understanding of the purpose of mortality, they have come up with some unusual explanations for our existence here on the earth. Man has always sought rational explanations for his circumstances, and you and I might have come to those same conclusions if we did not have the perspective of our existence that a loving Father has made available to us through living prophets. Let's review some basic truths of our existence as they relate to our sexual desires, and consider how differently some of your friends, teachers, or favorite television heroes might act if only they could see as you see.

The Purpose of Life

1. We have always existed.
2. We were born of a Heavenly Father and Mother into a spirit existence.
3. In that spirit existence we progressed until we were given the opportunity to come to earth to gain a physical body in the

image of our heavenly parents, and gain experience *away* from their direct influence.

4. With a veil over our minds restricting our memory of pre-mortal existence, we are now in the midst of our testing period, with one major goal—to learn the truth and live it.

5. The essence of that truth is found in the principles and ordinances of the gospel, made possible through the atonement of Jesus Christ. Obedience to these principles and ordinances will lead us to establish a family through a proper sequence of court-ship, marriage, and parenthood.

6. Those who learn to love as the Savior loved will be re-warded by eventually becoming like our heavenly parents—that is, we will have glorified, resurrected bodies, and we will become heavenly parents ourselves.

The purpose of life, then, is to learn to become like God, and the greatest school of instruction available to us is the family. Marriage and parenthood become more than just "our choice of life-styles," for they are the very essence of our purpose for being. Almost every man and woman will have the opportunity to marry and have children. In fact, marriage and parenthood make up one of the major tests of life in determining our fitness for the eternal possibilities that lie ahead. (Those denied these privileges due to circumstances over which they have no control have been prom-ised repeatedly that marriage and parenthood experiences await them if they are faithful. Indeed, for some that may be the supreme test of mortality—to postpone the realization of that desire.)

Elder Boyd K. Packer has expressed the central role that sexual relationships play in achieving our life's purpose:

> There was provided in our bodies—and this is sacred—a power of creation, a light, so to speak, that has the power to kindle other lights. This gift was to be used only within the sacred bonds of marriage. Through the exercise of this power of creation, a mortal body may be conceived, a spirit enter into it, and a new soul born into this life.
>
> This power is good. It can create and sustain family life, and it is in family life that we find the fountains of happiness. . . .

The power of creation—or we may say procreation—is not just an incidental part of the plan: it is essential to it. Without it, the plan could not proceed. The misuse of it may disrupt the plan. . . .

This creative power carries with it strong desires and urges. You have felt them already in the changing of your attitudes and your interests.

As you move into your teens, almost of a sudden a boy or girl becomes something new and intensely interesting. You will notice the changing of form and feature in your own body and in others. You will experience the early whispering of physical desire.

It was necessary that this power of creation have at least two dimensions: one, it must be strong; and two, it must be more or less constant.

This power must be strong, for most men by nature seek adventure. Except for the compelling persuasion of these feelings, men would be reluctant to accept the responsibility of sustaining a home and a family. This power must be constant, too, for it becomes a binding tie in family life. (*New Era*, July 1972, pp. 4-5.)

I love those words I have just quoted from Elder Packer. I hope you have read his entire talk, "Why Stay Morally Clean?" It may be the finest single statement on this sacred subject.

Do you remember the young lady's comment earlier in this chapter? Why didn't the Lord cause our bodies to mature sexually *after* marriage instead of when we're young teenagers? Without the sexual development of early adolescence, we would likely not be interested in marriage at age twenty or twenty-five. Don't you see that the Lord has given us those wonderful, frustrating teen years to learn about our bodies and emotions, to learn to feel comfortable with the opposite sex, and finally to develop a mature love for that certain one with whom we will begin our eternal family? If that sex drive were not present during our youth, it would set us behind at least a decade in our preparation for the greatest experience of mortality—marriage and parenthood.

Possibly there is another reason for our sexual development in early adolescence. The power of procreation, given at an early age, is a test for our physical body and spirit—one of the first major tests of our life. To be able to remain clean as we walk down the

5

road of life for ten or more years with that power, and with the desire to use it, is one of life's great tests of obedience and trust. If you can be trusted now, you will be trusted later—and with much more! The Lord knows you are old enough to prepare yourself to use that sacred power in a loving marriage relationship.

The Meaning of Chastity

The tentative title of this book was *The Case for Chastity*. Let's talk about that word *chastity* for just a moment. One of my institute students, a very bright returned missionary, reacted to my mention of the possible title of the book with: "Oh, no! That sounds too . . . too serious . . . too harsh. How about *The Case for Morality* or something like that?" Possibly your past experience and learning have conditioned your reaction to the word, too. My earliest recollection of the word *chastity* is associated with the white-haired prophet of my teenage years, President David O. McKay: "Be chaste, young men, it is the source of virile manhood." Chastity related closely to words like *purity, clean, unsullied, noble,* and *God.* I liked the word as a young person, and I still have those feelings when I think about it today.

But what does it mean? In Mutual or priesthood meeting we never had any problems with rowdiness or talkativeness when the subject of the lesson was chastity, because that meant we were going to talk about *sex.* And boy, did we want to know about sex! Sometimes we didn't like to admit we wanted to talk about it (or should I say *listen* about it, as the teacher or the bishop did all the talking), and I am sure that we didn't fully understand *why* we wanted to talk about it. But we were intensely interested in sorting out the conflicting information and feelings to which we were being exposed; and we knew it related to our physical bodies and the thoughts associated with those bodies. (I suppose the girls had similar feelings, but I somehow had the impression that they already understood and had *that* subject all figured out.)

My dictionary defines *chastity* as "the state or quality of being chaste or pure." Chaste is defined as "morally pure, decent, modest, abstaining from unlawful sexual intercourse, virtuous." (I couldn't help noticing that the word *chasten,* which I understood to mean "punish or scold," also means "to refine, to purify: to chasten one's style." Think of that in terms of how an unchaste person again becomes chaste. Steve Gilliland defines chastity as "the disciplining of our sexual desires and behaviors and the gaining of full understanding and control of self in all areas relating to sexuality" ("Chastity: A Principle of Power," *Ensign,* June 1980, p. 17).

As appropriate as the dictionary definition of chastity might be, something's missing. President Spencer W. Kimball felt it was necessary to be quite frank, even at the risk of offending those of pure sensitivities, in order to make sure every young person understood the meaning of unchastity as well as chastity. He refers to such premarital sexual experiences as passionate kissing, necking, petting, fornication (sexual intercourse by the unmarried), and preoccupation with sex in one's thoughts and speech as examples of unchaste behavior. Furthermore, he condemns sexual perversions such as masturbation (self-abuse), exhibitionism, homosexuality, and incest (sexual relations between persons so closely related that they are forbidden by law to marry). I recommend President Kimball's outstanding article, "President Kimball Speaks Out on Morality" (*New Era,* Nov. 1980, pp. 38-46).

In a thoughtful essay entitled "The Virtue of Chastity," John MacMurray expands the traditional definition of chastity. He writes of *external* chastity, refraining from sexual intercourse outside of marriage, and then outlines his broader view of chastity to include the sincere expression of our *inner* feelings. He suggests that a person who says he loves another when he does not sincerely feel that way is an emotionally insincere person — an unchaste person. Furthermore, if a married couple were to engage in sexual relations for selfish reasons outside of the context of genuine love, this would have to be termed unchaste or immoral.

One example of emotional insincerity helps us to appreciate his definition of chastity as it applies to modern life: "I can think of no other word which will express what I feel about the majority of cinema films and modern novels. They are unchaste; they arouse feelings that one doesn't really feel, by pretending emotions that the author doesn't feel." (In *The Case Against Pornography*, ed. David Holbrook [La Salle, Ill.: Library Press, 1973], p. 76.)

It might be helpful, then, to distinguish between two aspects of chastity. External chastity, the letter of the law, is to refrain from sexual practices outside of a marriage relationship. Internal chastity includes the development of inner purity, integrity, and oneness with God as a result of pure thoughts, motives, and desires. Inner chastity is known only to two — ourselves and God.

Two Important Keys

In writing this book, I intend to convince my readers that the chaste life-style, both before and after marriage, is the only kind of living that makes any kind of sense — now or in eternity. Let me suggest that to fully appreciate this conclusion we must ponder two terms — *eternal perspective* and *self-control*.

"Eye hath not seen, nor ear heard, neither have entered into the heart of man, the things which God hath prepared for them that love him" (1 Corinthians 2:9). We must recognize that there is a purpose in the Lord's plan for man beyond that which we are capable of fully understanding, except through the eyes of the Spirit. Even then, we get only glimpses; or as Paul says, "we see through a glass, darkly" (1 Corinthians 13:12). Keep in mind that we are all children — dependent, in part, on a heavenly parent who can see where we are headed better than we ourselves can. As we gain that perspective and accept it as our own, we must not lose sight of it, even for a moment. Later in this book I will share some ideas as to how you can keep that perspective.

What about self-control? It's not a popular word in today's vocabulary. The crux of the dilemma before us is one of self-control versus self-gratification. Stop and think for a minute of how many decisions you make in a typical day that revolve around the question of whether you will do what satisfies you *now*, or whether you will delay gratification and do what is best for another. Don't let anyone deceive you. Self-confidence, self-esteem, and self-control are all related, and they are not mere words. A victory in self-control is truly delicious, one of life's sweet and even exhilarating moments. Don't let anyone rob you of tasting that fruit—and it often tastes best when the temptation toward self-gratification has been the greatest.

You have heard all the arguments: "Why is it so wrong in some circumstances if it is so right in others?" "How can a ten-minute wedding ceremony make such a difference?" "It's not lustful, just natural." While serving in Florida on a mission and lecturing in a college history class, I mentioned the Church's emphasis on sexual purity. An outgoing and obviously liberal-minded young man raised his hand and blurted out, "Are you telling me that you two guys are going without sex for two years?" When I replied in the affirmative and added, "Not only for two years, but until marriage," he looked at his friends, shook his head in disbelief, and was silent.

Far too much emphasis is given by society to the role of sex. It is hoped that this book will not add to that overemphasis, but rather will help you to place your sexual self in proper perspective for your present and eternal happiness. Your physical desires are both necessary and wholesome. It's the circumstance under which they are gratified that is the key. If you finish this book, I hope you will be able to answer satisfactorily in your own mind and heart these four questions:

Why is it so hard for so many to be chaste?
Why is it so necessary that we be chaste?
What can we do to become chaste?
What can we do to ensure that we remain chaste?

You will need to rely upon reason, experience, and faith to answer them. Your experience is your own, but you can also benefit from the experiences of others included in this book, and I will share with you some of the logical reasons for remaining chaste. However, the greatest challenge is to develop your faith and spiritual sensitivity to the point that the path becomes clear—so clear, in fact, that you can see forever.

2

The Essential Seventh

Brother Foster had a unique ability to relate to teenagers. Few teachers could inspire and motivate young people to read and study in the scriptures as he could. Although "over the hill" at age thirty-one, he retained his ability to think (and occasionally act) like the students he taught in seminary each day. He would compete with them in a scripture chase contest in the morning, and defend his home from an expertly planned "TP" attack at midnight.

Today Brother Foster is not even a member of the Church. He has been excommunicated for adultery. The details of the story are personal and painful, but one great lesson emerges: *We cannot break the law of chastity and expect that life will go on unchanged!* Indeed, any degree of tampering with the powers of procreation will affect every other aspect of our lives. Our success in school or work, our relationship with friends and family, our goals and plans for the future, our ability to grow and progress in any undertaking we could possibly imagine, will be influenced positively or negatively by our moral status.

In the case of Brother Foster, the initial transgression occurred ten years earlier, just before he was married. As happens to many otherwise faithful couples, the intimacies during their engagement resulted in fornication. The temptation to excuse themselves and proceed to the temple, having confessed only to the Lord, set the stage for the failure of their marriage. By leaving out the bishop, the Lord's "Judge in Israel," fearing the embarrassment of confession or the possible postponement of obtaining the temple recommend, they grossly underestimated the seriousness of the sin. They undoubtedly rationalized that they could take care of it themselves. They were wrong, and the wound festered for years, interfering with their ability to grow together in love and trust. As children were born, and the cares of parenthood made it more difficult to cultivate their attraction for each other, Brother Foster sought his primary satisfactions away from home — in his work and hobbies. An extended business trip, loneliness, and the deep gnawing within of his unworthiness, led him to commit adultery, compounding the seriousness of the earlier transgression. Again, he tried to go on in life as though nothing had happened.

Opportunities to "serve in the kingdom" came. Being gifted with talents and abilities to relate to youth, he was invited to teach seminary. He had found his niche in life. Nothing in his previous experience satisfied him as did teaching young people. If only he could forget those past experiences. Wouldn't the Lord forgive him if he gave his whole life to helping youth? He was particularly successful in teaching his students about the importance of repentance, and getting young people who had committed serious moral transgression to visit with their bishops so that they could go forward in their lives unfettered and free.

While his rapport with youth and success in teaching grew, his marriage gradually disintegrated. He and his wife both kept up appearances before their families, their ward, and in other social settings, but both knew that their marriage was a sham. There was no eternal companionship in view — only darkness, heartache, and guilt. All that remained was facing up to the fact that the divorce would also remove the one source of happiness in Brother Foster's life — teaching young people.

Another woman came on the scene at this time to provide the catalyst for the complete breakdown of Brother Foster's marriage, and his life. With no companion to turn to for strength, and with past transgressions still unresolved, what additional harm could be done by seeking solace in the arms of one so understanding? The sin in seriousness next to murder was committed a third time, and repeated until separation and filing for divorce finally brought the situation to the attention of his priesthood leaders. Appointments were made; interviews resulted in a Church court; and Brother Foster found himself not only without his family but also without membership in the kingdom of God, and the accompanying loss of priesthood and the gift of the Holy Ghost.

If Brother Foster had been a lawyer rather than a seminary teacher, he likely could have continued his practice, for the world is very tolerant of sin today. I contend, however, that his practice would have been negatively affected — and it would have been a self-imposed deterioration of his ability, not simply the result of community displeasure toward his private life. This would be true regardless of his occupation.

Obeying the Word of Wisdom Is Not Enough!

What I want to stress by relating the story of Brother Foster and in the pages that follow, is simply this: *We cannot obey or disobey gospel principles in isolation.* That is, failure to live one principle invariably retards our progress in other areas of our lives. This is especially critical in dealing with moral worthiness. Elder Neal A. Maxwell refers to chastity as a center strand of the interwoven ecology of morality, which if unraveled hastens the unraveling of all the rest (see "Looking Beyond the Mark," an address presented at the Phi Kappa Phi banquet, 30 March 1976, at Brigham Young University).

Obedience to the Word of Wisdom, honest payment of tithes and offerings, regular scripture study, temple attendance, and faithful Church service do not alter the fact that breaking the law of chastity will cause the Spirit of the Lord to leave us. We are then left to cope with life's challenges without the assistance of the third member of the Godhead. Do you see what that can do to our efforts to live the gospel and succeed in our life's goals? We pray,

13

but we get little direction. We pay tithing, but do we receive the same spiritual benefits? We accept opportunities to serve in the Church, but do we feel the full spirit of our calling?

This is not to suggest that we need to become perfect in all aspects of gospel living before the Lord can bless us. On the contrary, every righteous act or intent of the heart is a blessing to us and others, but we limit our capacity to enjoy and benefit from that blessing when we do not have the Spirit of the Lord with us in abundance.

If all that we have just reviewed is true, it should not surprise us that the Church would go to such great lengths to help us avoid sexual transgression and maintain our purity. Can you visualize how odd it must seem to those who do not share our perspective, that we require our bishops and stake presidents to conduct regular, searching interviews with young people, with people called to serve in positions of leadership, and those desiring to perform ordinances in the sacred temples? In such interviews we voluntarily answer intimate questions regarding our thoughts and actions as they relate to chastity. The world finds it almost absurd that we hold Church courts that occasionally result in literally "blotting names off the records of the Church" in order to maintain the minimum standards of purity required of the Lord's covenant people.

Furthermore, sacrament meeting talks, firesides, seminary and institute lessons, articles in Church periodicals, and conference addresses continually keep us in remembrance of how infinitely important it is to use the sacred powers of procreation for the purposes which the Lord intended. The scriptures clearly identify virtue and purity as foundation stones upon which a full and abundant life must be built.

As we grow older, we soon learn that everyone has weaknesses, but it is important to understand that certain sins have a greater potential for harm than others. Simply stated, it is infinitely more important to have brakes than it is to have window glass in your car. It might be inconvenient to drive in a storm or in cold weather without a window, but it is *critical* that the brakes function properly! Failure to obey the Word of Wisdom, pay a full tithe, or failure to do home teaching regularly will all bring about a loss of certain blessings; but failure to live the law of chastity could jeopardize every aspect of our lives.

Isn't it possible that getting along with our family, enjoying a Church calling, finding inspiration in scripture study, advancing in a profession, feeling a desire to do missionary work, meeting our financial commitments, or disciplining ourselves to follow an exercise program, are all, in some degree, related to our ability to have clean thoughts?

I believe that there are negative consequences for breaking the law of chastity which cannot be seen or measured and, of course, cannot be identified in this book. Paul may have alluded to these when he spoke of "things which are seen" and "things which are not seen" that "are eternal" (2 Corinthians 4:18). The height of immaturity is to consider only the temporary or immediate consequences of a particular choice. Regret is nearly always the result of shortsightedness. In the chapters that follow, you will be presented with many reasons for living a pure life. But remember, there may be some *unseen* reasons that would make all the difference in the world—if we only knew them. Immoral thoughts or actions disqualify us from the very key to understanding those eternal reasons: the Spirit.

God Ordained Sex

This chapter would not be complete unless we concluded with a reminder of the fact that God ordained sex. He is the one who placed within us the organs and physical desires for a wise and eternal purpose. Too often, conditioning by our society makes it very difficult to be objective about this subject. Satan has brought about this condition, taking that which is most sacred—and which has the potential to bring us the greatest joy that man can experience—and reducing it to the level of pure physical gratification, or even worse, an animalistic perversion of divine power.

President Spencer W. Kimball speaks of two purposes of the sex act: to bring children into the world, and to express the love and unity felt between a husband and wife (see addresses in the *Ensign,* May 1974, p. 7; and Oct. 1975, p. 4). Brigham Young said that "every instinct in us is for a wise purpose in God when properly regulated and restrained, and guided by the Holy Spirit and kept within its proper legitimate bounds" (*Journal of Discourses,* 26:217).

In marriage, the sexual union fulfills the purposes of God, in providing the means for spirits to come to earth to gain physical bodies; in allowing two, who love each other totally, to express that love physically; and in providing a context where godlike traits of self-control, unselfishness, kindness, and consideration can be developed. Those who deny themselves the full realization of these divine purposes by tampering improperly or prematurely with the sexual powers will find the loss of these blessings to be bitter. Those who cultivate purity and chastity in thought and action will, on the other hand, be rewarded tenfold.

An old wives' tale speaks of a mother kneeling by her child's cradle to pray. As she prayed, she heard the voices of angels. She felt the fluttering of angel wings, and when she looked up, she saw five angels hovering in the air over the cradle of her child. The first one said, "I am the Angel of Wealth. Whomsoever I touch shall never know want." The second angel said, "I am the Angel of Health, and whomsoever I touch shall never know pain." The third said, "I am the Angel of Fame, and whomsoever I touch shall be world renowned." The fourth said, "I am the Angel of Knowledge, and whomsoever I touch shall have the wisdom of the ages." But the fifth said, "I am none of these. I am the Angel of High Ideals." And the mother put forth her hands and said, "Oh, you of High Ideals, touch my child."

I recall an incident in my youth when I was feeling somewhat unimportant because, to me, I lacked all the essential qualities for being popular at my junior high school in Des Moines, Iowa. I had to wear thick glasses; I was always second string instead of a starter; and one of the popular cheerleaders once referred to me as "that new kid, 'what's his name.' " I went home teaching with Brother Burdick (who reminded me of President David O. McKay because of his wavy white hair), and he gave a brief lesson to each of our families on the importance of being clean in thought and action. As we were riding home, he looked at me and said, "Larry, if you do nothing else of importance in this life but be morally clean, you will be counted one of the great men of our time."

3

Lusts of the Flesh

He was the kind of missionary companion you'd like to have while tracting in a tough neighborhood. Elder Doe stood out at zone conference because of his sheer bulk, but was mild-mannered and even shy to the point of allowing his companions to nearly always take the lead in meeting people. He had a great family supporting him at home, and all who worked closely with him in the mission field enjoyed his quiet steadiness.

What could possibly have led him to leave his apartment late one night, commit a serious crime, and wait for the police to come and arrest him? Eventually the judge returned him to the custody of his father to return home on the condition that he get psychiatric help.

I suppose most assumed that Elder Doe had just suffered an emotional breakdown due to the rigors and stress of missionary life. There was another factor that was known only to a few. When his mission president recognized that he would not be returning to his apartment to continue his missionary work, he sent some elders to gather his clothes and other personal belongings and bring them to the mission home. Under the mattress they found a stack of explicitly pornographic magazines. When the mission president confronted Elder Doe about the magazines, he broke down and cried, revealing more sorrow and tears than he had since the entire incident began. Why would a young man be more embarrassed by the revelation of his reading habits than his arrest for burglary?

It was the opinion of at least one analyst that Elder Doe was unable to function in his missionary responsibilities because he lacked the Spirit of the Lord. The loss of the Spirit was caused by his addiction to pornography. This addiction resulted from years of exposure to a warped set of values, perpetrated through magazines, books, and movies that misrepresented the purpose of the sexual drive. When the shame of his hypocrisy became more than he could bear, he preferred to be sent home dishonorably for a felony and emotional breakdown rather than admit the basic source of his problem to his parents, priesthood leaders, and mission president. Such is the influence that Satan can wield through misdirecting the sacred sexual powers.

That society has seriously deteriorated morally is an understatement. Those old enough to compare the behavior and values of today with the standards of just a decade or two ago, are painfully aware that young people face some unique challenges in maintaining high standards of chastity. Evil has always been present in any society or time, but never has it been so blatantly available, encouraged, and even advocated as the "healthy" way to live.

IN the World, but Not OF the World

I think it would help if I carefully defined a term that is used often in the Church. Have you ever heard that "we must learn to be *in* the world without being *of* the world?" That neatly sums up the challenge you and I face today.

The "world" in the first sense means this physical, mortal place where we live—the earth, our nation, our community. We are all *in* the world whether we like it or not, but we need not be *of* the world. The "world" in the latter sense describes the behavior and values of many people living in this world. The scriptures use another term to describe the same concept: *Babylon*. The "world" or "Babylon" means anything which is contrary to the kind of life our Heavenly Father would have us live while we are here on earth. It is that which distracts us from becoming pure so that we can eventually behold the face of Christ and abide the day of his coming.

Elder Neal A. Maxwell made an interesting statement: "There is a premium in breaking away from the world as quickly as we can. Youth are doing it sooner today than most of us did in our day." (Church Educational System [CES] Area Directors Convention, Apr. 1981.) He implies that we all have a little bit of the "world" with us, but that we ought to "break away" from it as soon as possible. Some are apparently doing a pretty good job, but others seemingly enjoy the world too much to want to break away. Why is it so hard to leave? Why is it necessary that we turn our back on the world?

James, the Lord's brother, says that "friendship with the world is enmity [hostility] with God" (James 4:4), and "a double minded man is unstable in all his ways" (James 1:8). The Lord himself said it most emphatically: "No man can serve two masters: for either he will hate the one, and love the other; or else he will hold to the one, and despise the other. Ye cannot serve God and Mammon." (Matthew 6:24.) Mammon is usually translated to mean worldly wealth, but the same principle would apply to any worldly influence. I am suggesting that you must not think it unusual when you differ with many of your friends, teachers, or prominent people of the world in regard to what is right and what is wrong, what is proper and what is improper.

Melanie attended the senior prom, dressed in a fashionable, backless, low-cut formal dress. She was enjoying herself very much until she bumped into her bishop at a nice restaurant following the dance. Although he was very happy to see her, she wished desperately for a shawl that would cover her nakedness. Seeing her bishop had suddenly brought her back to the reality of who she really was—a child of God housed in a mortal tabernacle, a temple for her spirit.

We cannot serve two masters. Remember Elder Maxwell's statement: *"There is a premium in breaking away from the world as quickly as we can."*

After we describe some of the reasons our modern society makes it difficult to live a chaste life, I hope you will see the need to examine your own values and create the kind of environment you want for yourself. Despite how negative or contrary to God's purposes the world around us may be, we need to understand that we can create a climate now that prepares us to feel comfortable for eternity. Perhaps feeling too comfortable in this present world may cause us to be most uncomfortable in that better (and permanent) world ahead of us. Can you imagine a society with no lust, no immoral or suggestive entertainment, no jokes with double meanings, no perversion? Does that sound like the kind of world you would enjoy? It's so hard to try to live in both worlds. We must make a choice or remain double-minded, frustrated people.

Let's take a quick look at a few of the special challenges in our world. I have selected just a few that will serve to make the point that we must not depend on those who do not understand the gospel perspective to shape our values and behavior. We must be awake and alert, for the hazards are *not* clearly labeled "Warning! May be dangerous to your spiritual health!"

Changing Standards of Morality

I don't want to mislead you into thinking that the problem of unchastity is a modern one, for every generation has struggled to understand and discipline the sexual nature. One social scientist noted that "in 2,000 years, the Western World has not succeeded in bringing to adulthood as virgins the majority of males in even one generation" (Ira Reiss, in *The Individual, Sex, and Society,* ed. Carlfred Broderick and Jessie Bernard [Baltimore: The Johns Hopkins Press, 1969], p. 112). We might question the accuracy of that statement or his ability to verify it, but it is evident that it has always been a challenge to maintain a high standard of sexual morality in any society.

God has always prohibited sexual intercourse outside of lawful marriage. Western civilization (thanks to the Judeo-Christian tradition) has generally adopted the ideal of chastity, but in practice has tolerated a double-standard, which in essence required strict chastity for women but allowed young men to "sow their wild oats." Also helping to maintain the chastity standard were the triple terrors of "infection, conception, and detection." Fear of venereal disease, pregnancy, and loss of reputation kept sexual practice somewhat under the rug for the young.

Today the so-called new morality is being proclaimed from college lectern to church pulpit. Many have rejected the religious and cultural prohibitions of the ages and developed their own set of moral assumptions regarding sexual practices. Crying for the elimination of the double standard, women have demanded equal rights to be immoral. The playboy philosophy is described by one advocate as a "natural right for the individual to be principally concerned with himself" (Hugh Hefner, quoted in Wayland Young, *Eros Denied* [New York: Grove Press, 1964], p. 28).

Many liberal-minded ministers and theologians are joining the mad rush toward gratification. Dr. Joseph Fletcher, formerly of the Episcopal Theological School, Cambridge, Massachussetts, rocked the field of Christian behavior during the 1960s with his philosophy of "situation ethics." The following excerpt from an interview with Dr. Fletcher illustrates the position of many today:

> Put into practical terms, situation ethics challenges the entire order of Christian conduct. Premarital sex is one example: "The Bible clearly affirms sex as a high-order value, at the same time sanctioning marriage (although not always monogamy), but any claim that the Bible requires sex to be expressed solely within marriage is only an inference. There is nothing explicitly forbidding premarital acts," says Dr. Fletcher.
>
> Premarital sex, until recently, was not the "loving thing to do," according to Dr. Fletcher. . . . Today, however, contraceptives and modern medicine can be combined with a loving attitude to make such acts morally acceptable, contends Dr. Fletcher. Since 40 percent of the sexually mature population is single, argues Dr. Fletcher, confining sex to married couples is no longer practical in many situations. (*Memphis Press-Scimitar*, 14 Feb. 1976.)

Seeking justification to ignore the "Do's and Don'ts" and "Thou Shalt Nots," and other absolutes of the past, many have embraced the commandment to love one another as the only meaningful basis for determining the rightness or wrongness of behavior. Now on the surface, this sounds like an appropriate standard for guiding our lives. Such philosophies can be convincing with catch phrases like "love is the final judge" or "people are more important than standards." The problem comes in applying such philosophies to real-life situations. When people ignore the specific commandments and experience of the past, behaviors that initially seem loving often turn out to be most unloving.

Unfortunately, when permissive values are taught from many respected sources of authority in a society (such as teachers, ministers, media personalities, scientists, etc.), they tend to acquire a validity that has no basis in fact or experience. They merely reflect the personal desires of those perpetuating the values. Youth are often confused when they hear one thing from their parents or seminary teacher, and just the opposite from their sociology teacher or the expert on the television talk show. (See chapters 5 and 6 for a detailed explanation of just how such a philosophy crumbles in reality. I also recommend a book by Victor L. Brown, Jr., entitled *Human Intimacy: Illusion and Reality* [Salt Lake City: Parliament Publishers, 1981] as a fine statement in reply to those who argue for permissiveness.)

The Entertainment Media

When I was a young boy, I attended every movie that came to the Star Theater in Fairfield, Montana. Every Friday evening my brother and sisters and I were given twenty-five cents to get into the movie and buy a treat. I cannot recall my parents ever questioning me or being concerned about the movie that might have been playing.

How well I recall seeing *Gone with the Wind*. In that memorable scene Rhett Butler turned to Scarlett O'Hara and said (in reply to her concern about what she would do if he were to leave her), "Frankly, my dear, I don't give a damn." At that moment, an involuntary gasp was heard from that collective body of mid-1950s moviegoers. That was the first swear word any of us had heard in a movie or television show. I need not describe the change that has taken place in just a few decades. Needless to say, few people today attend *every* movie shown at their local theater; and only a negligent parent would fail to carefully investigate the movies available to children today.

The daily dosage of immodesty, profanity, and perversion in the media (television, movies, radio, magazines and books, advertisements, and music) makes it nearly impossible to totally isolate ourselves from these influences. So widespread has the emphasis on sexual gratification become, that it has attained a degree of respectability in our society among those who shape public attitude and opinion. I speak of newscasters, editors, entertainment celebrities, political leaders, and even ministers. Those who object to these trends tend to be labeled intolerant prudes, dismissed as reactionaries, or accused of seeking to deny freedom of speech.

The PG-rated movie that caters to the baser instincts in man may do as much harm as the X-rated "adults only" films, because most who are seeking to live a chaste life will avoid the obviously pornographic film, while rationalizing to themselves that the PG-rated movie really isn't that bad — just a few poor scenes. Unfortunately, it is that scene or two that often dominates the mental processes during the movie and for days after. Many of us have experienced the Friday or Saturday evening movie date that effectively dampens our spirituality for the entire weekend. Unfortunately, many of those movies that distract us from our course are now viewed in our own homes, uncensored, through cable television and home video players, slowly and surely driving away the Spirit of the Lord from the last place of defense.

Most of us have not had the experience of viewing a truly pornographic movie. We would do well to remain innocent and curious rather than to give in to the temptation. I recall bumping into a friend I had not seen in several years. As we talked and reminisced, the conversation turned to the fact that he had recently changed his employment, which had necessitated moving to another state. One of the reasons for leaving his former employer was the fact that he traveled extensively and was away from home more than he liked. Initially he remained in the motel room each evening, reading or watching television, while the other salesmen he worked with visited the lounge or the theater. After a period of time he began to go with them to the movies, and on one occasion his curiosity got the best of him and he attended an X-rated movie. It was so explicit in its perversions that even months later, as he was conversing with me, he still had to force the mental images out of his mind.

Like Elder Doe with the pornographic magazines, many adults and youth become addicted to the perversions available at every turn, only to find that the temporary pleasure these seem to provide turns to bitter ashes, leaving guilt, regret, and loss of the strength needed for true fulfillment.

The negative intent and effect of some popular music has been well documented. (See Elder Boyd K. Packer, "Worthy Music — Worthy Thoughts," *Ensign*, Jan. 1974, pp. 25-27; and Lex de Azevedo, "The Effect of Music on Our Lives," devotional speech at Ricks College, 2 Feb. 1982.) A youth who ignores those realities and refuses to be selective in what he listens or dances to is only hurting himself. Much of the harm done by an exclusive diet of popular music results from missing the cultural benefits of other types of music that lift and inspire. The effort necessary to appreciate the value of enduring forms of musical expression is expended by relatively few, especially in a day of emphasis on physical, rather than spiritual, experience.

Regarding literature, it is becoming more difficult to find reading that enobles, rather than debases man. Despite the flood of books and magazines that inundate the popular market, it may be more challenging to find good reading material than ever before. Many who pride themselves on turning away from the "boob tube" spend endless hours reading "escape" novels of romance or violence. We may argue that such reading is done only for relaxation or pleasure, yet the net effect is no different than the influence of the television or the theater. T. S. Eliot reminds us that "it is just the literature that we read for 'amusement' or 'purely for pleasure' that may have the greatest and least suspected influence upon us. It is the literature which we read with the least effort that can have the easiest and most insidious influence on us." (*Selected Essays* [New York: Harcourt, Brace, 1950], p. 350.)

Have you ever heard it said that what you do or think about in your free time says more about your character than any other activity? If that is true, the books we read for pleasure, the kind of movies we attend, and the music we select for our enjoyment will shape our thought patterns, affect our behavior, and determine our values and goals more than our schooling, jobs, or attendance at church. Possibly, such choices merely reflect back to us what is truly important in our life.

Immodesty

Another modern problem that prevents many from attaining a higher state of purity is the low standard of dress and modesty in our society. Listen to the counsel of a modern prophet on this subject. He is very direct:

> The young people today seem to talk about sex glibly. They hear it in the locker rooms and on the street, they see and hear it in shows and on television, they read it in the pornographic books everywhere. Those who do not resist this influence absorb and foster it. The spirit of immodesty has developed until nothing seems to be sacred.
>
> One factor contributing to immodesty and the breakdown of moral values is the modern dress worn by our young women and their mothers. I see young women, and some older ones, on the streets wearing shorts. This is not right. The place for women to wear shorts is in their rooms, in their own homes, in their own gardens. I see some of our LDS mothers, wives, and daughters wearing dresses extreme and suggestive in style. Even some fathers encourage it. I wonder if our sisters realize the temptation they are flaunting before men when they leave their bodies partly uncovered or dress in tight-fitting, body-revealing, form-fitting sweaters.
>
> . . . A woman is most beautiful when her body is properly clothed and her sweet face adorned with her lovely hair. She needs no more attractions. (Spencer W. Kimball, *The Miracle of Forgiveness* [Salt Lake City: Bookcraft, 1969], p. 226.)

27

President Kimball asks if young women realize how their dress styles affect young men. There are possibly two reasons why a young lady would wear a bikini bathing suit, or a suggestive, form-revealing article of clothing. First, she may not realize what she is doing. She may be completely innocent of any wrong intent; she may be woefully ignorant regarding the influence her dress style has on the young men with whom she may associate. If this be the case, she needs to be *educated*. The other possible reason is that she knows *well* what effect her dress has on the young men that may see her. She is playing the role of the temptress if she knowingly seeks to entice those who may see her; and in that case she needs to *repent!*

Phil called for his favorite girl one summer evening. She beamed as she came to the door and twirled to show him the new dress she had bought for the dance—a bright, yellow sundress which accentuated her deep-tanned skin. At the dance, Phil was alternately attracted and repelled, for the low-cut neckline made it difficult for his girlfriend to maintain her modesty. He was physically attracted to her, but he also remembered that he would be leaving for his mission within a few months. Phil wanted very much to purify and prepare himself for the temple experience and the work that would follow.

He thought about it for several days, and finally found the right time to discuss it with her. He told her how attractive she was and how much he cared for her. Then he asked if she would do him a favor. "Would I be expecting too much to ask you not to wear that new yellow dress any more?" Her look of surprise, followed by an understanding twinkle in her eye, let him know that she understood without his having to explain in more detail. She cared for him as much as he did for her, so it was not hard for her to modify her dress style.

I am convinced that the majority of those young women who are somewhat careless in what they choose to wear are innocent of evil intent. Most just enjoy being a girl. However, girls, if you are still so naive as to conclude that the young men of your life look at you and what you wear in the same way as you look at yourself in the mirror, or in the same light that your father or brother looks at you, you are sorely in need of education. I am not speaking of young men with perverted minds or corrupt intent; I am speaking of the finest young men in the Church—those with strong desires to be pure, and to control their thoughts and actions. If you would be wise, clothe your beauty properly, so that his attraction to you will be based on more than merely physical arousal. In the future, as your physical endowments fade, as they most surely will, you will be loved for those infinitely more important (and enduring) qualities of the spirit and character.

Traditionally, immodesty in dress has not been a serious problem for young men; but our physically oriented society has changed all that. Today, the image makers have concluded that men, too, have the right to wear sexy clothing, jewelry, and hair styles. Hence the "macho" man of our time wears pants that are too tight for modesty, and shirts that expose the chest. He styles his hair so that admiring females can think of nothing but running their fingers through it, and wears cologne designed to bring out the animal passions of the opposite sex.

Furthermore, bare chests and hairy thighs in public are the norm for summer living for many of you young men. Yes, the heat can be uncomfortable, and we understand how important it is that you have that dark tan, but all of the same arguments we just used for the young ladies apply to you, too. This is a day of equal rights and equal responsibilities. These physical bodies that the Lord has given us are indeed beautiful and wondrous in what they can do, but the Creator has given guidelines and cautions that we must heed.

You have been reminded by parents, Church leaders, and others of the importance of modesty, but let me conclude this section with a suggestion: The vast majority of you who read this book hope to one day enter the holy temple to be personally endowed with power from on high, and be sealed for eternity to your spouse in marriage. When you leave the temple, you will be wearing the sacred garment of the Holy Priesthood. You have probably observed the shape of that garment on a parent or friend.

Just as you are seeking to prepare for the temple now through living the commandments of God, you should also prepare yourself now to maintain the Lord's standard of modesty in dress, by wearing only those clothes that you could wear with the temple garment. This would, of course, eliminate bare chests for boys, shorts and cut-off jeans for both, backless and sleeveless dresses for girls. There are times when it is appropriate to wear modest athletic or swimming suits, but except for those occasions you ought to look at yourself in the mirror before leaving home and ask yourself if you would feel comfortable if you happened to run into your bishop, the prophet, or even the Savior.

Be Vigilant and Alert

Everything we have discussed in this chapter has an effect on our thoughts and desires. As we struggle to control those thoughts and desires and become pure in heart, we sometimes assume that others in the Church do not have to worry so much about these matters; that we alone have the tendency toward thoughts that drag us down. I believe this is a rather universal challenge in and out of the Church, and we can take comfort in knowing that nearly everyone has been confronted by temptation in these areas, and faces a rather constant need to be vigilant and alert. (See chapter 9 for suggestions on managing your thoughts.)

You are all familiar with what addiction means. I hope you have not learned of addiction from experiencing it firsthand or observing it in the life of someone you love. Alcoholism and drug addiction cause more physical, emotional, and spiritual suffering than I care to document in this book. Let me suggest, however, that it is possible to become addicted to harmful practices and thoughts as well as harmful substances. Experimentation or curiosity in youth can lead to dependency and loss of free agency later in life. Physical appetites, when given a free rein, can become so powerful that one literally loses the will, desire, and ability to change. (See chapter 10 for helps in overcoming extreme addiction.)

Samuel the Lamanite taught that truth to the Nephites of 6 B.C. when he said: "But behold, your days of probation are past; ye have procrastinated the day of your salvation until it is everlastingly too late, and your destruction is made sure; . . . for ye have sought all the days of your lives for . . . happiness in doing iniquity" (Helaman 13:38; see also Mormon 2:12-15).

Many of those who teach you and lead you are, themselves, addicted to their physical passions, and thereby seek to justify and excuse their own behavior by teaching that such passions and practices are normal and good. You need to beware of the "experts" who have the titles, the degrees, and the positions that might cause you to place your trust in them. The scriptures teach that the Light of Christ (our conscience) is given to every man so that he has an almost instinctive morality regarding right and wrong. Unfortunately, it is possible to lose that light, as many have done; yet they continue to teach and influence others because of their temporal credentials. Mormon, the Nephite prophet, taught us that the surest way to judge between good and evil is through the Spirit of Christ (see Moroni 7:15-18). If those in positions of influence—the experts—have disqualified themselves from enjoying the Spirit of Christ, you are in a better position to judge than they. Trust your conscience, the whispering of the Spirit, or the teachings of those you know to have that Spirit. "For behold, my brethren, it is given unto you to judge, that ye may know good from evil; and the way to judge is as plain, that ye may know with a perfect knowledge, as the daylight is from the dark night" (Moroni 7:15).

4

Sawing Sawdust

"A newspaper editor, speaking to a college graduating class, asked, 'How many of you have ever sawed wood? Let's see your hands.' Many hands went up. Then he asked, 'How many of you have ever sawed sawdust?' No hands went up. 'Of course, you can't saw sawdust!' he exclaimed. 'It's already sawed! And it's the same with the past. When you start worrying about things that are over and done with, you're merely trying to saw sawdust.' " (Kenneth Higbee, "Forgetting Those Things Which Are Left Behind," *Ensign*, Sept. 1972, p. 83.)

Moral transgression often brings with it a double penalty. First, we suffer the actual consequences of the transgression itself; and second, even after forsaking the sin, many continue to suffer from their inability to forgive and forget—they try to saw sawdust. Lowell Bennion asks, "Why be defeated twice, once by our mistakes and again by our attitude toward them?" (*Improvement Era,* Oct. 1967, p. 12).

Guilt can be of two kinds. Appropriate guilt serves as the motivation to repent and improve. It serves much the same purpose as pain. A headache or other pain can warn the physical body that something is not right (improper diet, overexertion, etc.), just as guilt can warn the spiritual self that something is wrong. Pain ignored or tolerated can lead to serious health problems or death.

33

Guilt ignored or tolerated will often lead to spiritual decline or death.

However, after we have repented, we often continue to be plagued by our past. This feeling is not of God and can cripple our future efforts to progress. Continual brooding over mistakes often leaves us without the strength to resist temptation, and we find ourselves settling for standards that are far below our potential. The transgression, repeated, results in a vicious cycle of discouragement, poor self-esteem, and hopelessness.

Satan's Great Lie: "It's Too Late!"

We are taught that Satan "seeketh that all men might be miserable like unto himself" (2 Nephi 2:27). One of his most successful methods of increasing the number of miserable people in the world is to plant ideas into the minds of those who make mistakes—all of us—such as the following:

"It's too late for me. I've gone too far."

"Who would ever want me after what I've done?"

"What's the use of trying. I can't change the way I am."

"God would never want me in his kingdom."

When you feel those thoughts creeping into your consciousness, just remember that you can't find any of them in the scriptures. You will never hear a prophet, bishop, loving parent, or teacher planting such ideas in your head. That is because those ideas are from Satan, "the father of *lies*." The ultimate danger of this kind of thinking is that we tend eventually to lose all desire to repent and improve. We have the *power* to repent only as long as we have the *will* to repent. Can you think of a more miserable condition than that described by the prophet Mormon as "the sorrowing of the damned" (Mormon 2:13)? Elder Neal A. Maxwell refers to those Nephites as being "trapped in a kind of 'no man's land,' " because, although sin had ceased to give any pleasure, neither would they repent.

When you find yourself struggling with Satan's lies about repenting, think instead on these truths: God "will with the temptation make a way to escape, that ye may be able to bear it" (1 Corinthians 10:13); and "though your sins be as scarlet, they shall be as white as snow" (Isaiah 1:18). "I do not condemn you; go your ways and sin no more" (D&C 6:35), "forgetting those things which are behind, and reaching forth unto those things which are before" (Philippians 3:13).

The purpose of this chapter is to outline the beautiful promise of hope made available to us through the atonement of Jesus Christ.

All Will Eventually Repent (One Way or Another)

The Lord has commanded us to repent or suffer (see D&C 19:4). Did you read that carefully? He said repent *or* suffer, not repent *and* suffer. With the exception of those who commit the unpardonable sin, all mankind will be brought forth by the power of the resurrection to a degree of glory (see D&C 76:31-39). When we sin, we wound our spirits. Spiritual wounds must be healed before we are resurrected. How do we go about healing a wounded spirit? We have two choices. We can take advantage of the atonement of Christ and allow his suffering to heal us, or we can suffer for our own sins until our spirits are healed sufficiently to enter into a resurrected body and dwell in a kingdom of glory.

What will determine which kingdom of glory we find ourselves enjoying for eternity? Those who repent according to the Lord's prescribed plan will inherit the celestial kingdom. They will exercise faith in Christ sufficient to lead them to repent, enter into the covenant of baptism, receive the Holy Ghost and endure to the end (see D&C 76:50-70). *Celestial repentance* leads to a profound appreciation and sense of gratitude for God. It motivates us not only to turn away from evil and error but to reach out for all good. We receive the Holy Spirit as a guide toward perfection. It results in peace regarding our past life, coupled with a divine discontent that keeps us improving toward eternal life.

Terrestrial repentance results in harmony with mankind. Repentance is simply the right and ethical thing to do. It is based not so much on godly sorrow and recognition of Christ's cleansing power as it is on a human level of understanding that misses the whole point of sanctification and becoming godlike.

Telestial repentance is characterized by those who are "sorry" they got caught. They repent only because circumstances force them to change. They are practicing "pretendance" rather than "repentance"—pretending to be sorry. Those who refuse to repent in this life must suffer, even as Christ, which suffering was so intense as to cause "even God, the greatest of all, to tremble because of pain, and to bleed at every pore, and to suffer both body and spirit" (D&C 19:18).

Regardless of the level of our repentance, the significant fact is that Christ has already suffered and paid for the sins of all. He has "bought us with a price," an exquisite price that you and I cannot fully appreciate or understand. Godly sorrow results when we finally come to realize that some of that blood was shed for *us!*

The Lord's plan and desire is that we progress and grow through recognizing our mistakes, forsaking them, and pressing forward, having become a better and wiser person. His atonement —the greatest event in history—makes that possible. Our refusal to believe in ourselves or in Christ's ability to forgive is, in a sense, a denial of the entire plan of redemption, and indicates a need to ponder the very first principle of the gospel, faith in the Lord Jesus Christ. How might our Savior feel when he observes us suffering because we have sinned, when he has already suffered for those sins?

The Lord's Promise of Forgiveness

I would mislead you if I left you with the impression that repentance is easy. It is not my intention to minimize the seriousness of moral transgression and the difficult process required of those who desire eternal life. President Spencer W. Kimball has written:

> Those who, having committed grievous sexual sin, assume this sin to be unforgivable . . . are perhaps confusing difficulty with impossibility. Certainly the road of repentance from such sin is not easy, which is one good reason for abstaining in the first place. . . .
>
> To every forgiveness there is a condition. The plaster must be as wide as the sore. The fasting, the prayers, the humility must be equal to or greater than the sin. There must be a broken heart and a contrite spirit. There must be "sackcloth and ashes." There must be tears and genuine change of heart. There must be conviction of the sin,

abandonment of evil, confession of the error to properly constituted authorities of the Lord. There must be restitution and a confirmed, determined change of pace, direction, and destination. Conditions must be controlled and companionship corrected or changed. There must be a washing of robes to get them white and there must be a new consecration and devotion to the living of all the laws of God. In short, there must be an overcoming of self, of sin, and of the world. (*The Miracle of Forgiveness*, p. 353.)

One who is willing to pay the price of sincere and complete repentance speaks loud and clear to God, others, and himself. "I am a changed person! A new man! I am worthy!" It takes great courage and self-discipline to refrain from sexual temptation in the first place, and it takes similar courage and discipline to completely repent of moral transgression. Though it is better never to transgress (see the end of this chapter), the promise of the scriptures is clear — that forgiveness can be complete.

Probably a most difficult truth to understand, for those who transgress, is that God loves the person just as much after as he did before a transgression. I can't think of a single concept that is a greater inducement to repentance than the realization that we are unconditionally loved. The Savior taught this great truth in three parables recorded in Luke 15: "The Lost Sheep," "The Lost Coin," and "The Prodigal Son." I am profoundly moved by the mental image of the father watching daily for the return of his wayward son. When the young man finally "came to himself" and returned home, his father saw him from a great distance and "ran, and fell on his neck, and kissed him."

Our ability to recognize God's love for us, even when we seem so unlovable, is enhanced if we are fortunate to have an earthly father (or mother) who has demonstrated that kind of love. My own father was occasionally disappointed in my behavior as a boy, many times having to reprove me verbally or physically; but I never doubted that he loved me! Now, as a father of four sons and a daughter, I understand that at times a child's rebelliousness can even *increase* a father's love and compassion.

A second area of difficulty associated with the repentance process is the necessity of going to those we have offended to seek forgiveness. Satan works on our pride in such instances by convincing us that we need not make amends. It can be very painful to go to one we have offended and admit our change of heart. (Sometimes they have been our partners in sin and laugh at our penitence.)

The Lord has required confession to our bishop in the case of sexual sin, which can be a humbling experience. Those who cannot observe the confession requirement may not sufficiently understand the precariousness of their position, for if they did, they would look to the bishop in the same way as a man with a painful toothache looks to a dentist. While recovering from a back operation following my mission, I found myself waiting anxiously for the nurse to give the regular injections of pain killer. I can't recall ever looking forward to a shot before or since; but, of course, I had never been in such a state of constant pain. How do you spell relief? B-I-S-H-O-P!

Often the most difficult aspect of forgiveness is forgiving ourselves. This is closely intertwined with our recognition of God's love for us. Lowell Bennion tells the following impressive and true experience that illustrates the strength that can be derived from turning to God and his Son, Jesus Christ:

> I had an experience in the mission field that is very memorable to me. A man came to me after Church — he was twice my age, a very unhappy person — and told me that he had committed a grave sin before he joined the Church, that his wife would not forgive him, would not divorce him, and constantly reminded him of his good-for-nothingness. He said, "I've come to think of myself at her estimate. How can I be whole again and pure of heart, clean in my thoughts?" I said, "What have you tried to do for this problem?" He said, "I've fought it. I've fought it." I'd had a class in psychology before I went on a mission, and I told him there must be a better way than to fight sin. We knelt in prayer together, and afterwards I gave him a book to read — *As a Man Thinketh in His Heart, So Is He* — and then I put my arm around him (he was shorter than I), gave him a firm handclasp, and told him that he could overcome his problem. And then by inspiration or coincidence I said to him, "How would you like to prepare the Lord's supper for Sunday School?" (He was a teacher in the Aaronic Priesthood.) He said, "Do you think I'm worthy to do

38

this?" I said, "No, I don't think any of us really are. But I think Jesus would be pleased if you would render him this service." And so he proceeded to set the Lord's table each Sunday morning. After about six weeks I met him coming up the aisle before Sunday School. I put out my hand to reassure him. He put his hand behind his back and said nothing. I said, "Have I offended you?" He said, "Oh, no, I've just washed my hands with soap and hot water, and I can't shake hands with you or any man until I've set the Lord's table." That's the most beautiful reverence I've seen in that simple act of setting the Lord's table. And I said to myself, "Brother, it's getting to you." I was so pleased. In another six weeks he came to me after church again and said, "I'm a new man. I'm a new man."

Then I asked him to give a talk in church on some principle of the gospel of Christ that he really believed in and why. I kept him thinking about the Savior. Well, serving the Savior in a simple way and thinking about him during the week, this man became a new creature. It was beautiful. And I realized that I'd never used the Savior in my own life in the same way. I don't mind telling you that I did after that. I had the wonderful thrill of overcoming what I thought was a weakness in me by thinking of him and making him the center of my prayers and my life. (*New Era*, Nov. 1972, p. 16.)

You Can Change the Past!

I want to try to change a notion you have probably always accepted as true: that you can't change the past. I am thinking of an instance in my earlier life of which I am not especially proud. Can you think of something that happened five or more years ago you would just as soon forget? Now, as I think of my past experience, I can recall how badly I felt at the time. It consumed my thoughts and moods for days, even though I asked the Lord's forgiveness and committed myself never to repeat that sin. Gradually I began to accept the fact that I really had been forgiven, but that did not entirely erase the memory and my embarrassment, for it would occasionally return to my thoughts. Now, over two decades later, with a mission, marriage, family, and years of Church service in the interim, I can still recall the transgression; but I no longer feel the pangs of regret. Although I still wish I had not made the mistake, I can fully accept that I have matured, repented, progressed, and will not be held accountable for that sin if I continue in the proper course for the rest of my life.

It's all a matter of perspective. When we are close to an event, it looms large in our thoughts; but as time passes, it gradually diminishes in relation to new experiences. Can you picture a railroad track or highway extending behind you in a straight line? The telephone poles along the road seem to get smaller and smaller. We know they haven't changed in size, but their influence on our consciousness changes. So also our sins, if we properly repent, will gradually have less and less influence on our lives. The pull of old habits lessens with time. The pain of old transgressions is gradually removed. In that way, we can change the past. To the person who dwells on his sins by refusing to forgive himself or refusing to repent, the influence of sin will remain a dominant force, preventing growth and happiness.

Matthew Cowley used to say: "The good man—no matter how bad he is, or how low he has sunk—is the man who starts coming up. The bad man is the man, no matter how high he has reached in his goodness and morality, who begins to come down."

This perspective can be illustrated by the accompanying diagrams. Each depicts the relative progress toward perfection in an individual's life. Which would you prefer?

1. *Growth Toward Perfection* (One Year)

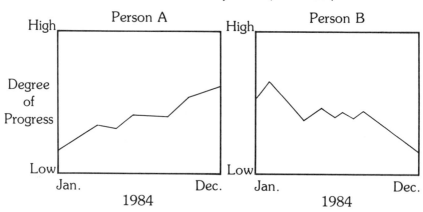

40

As you look at diagram 2, it becomes obvious that it is difficult to judge the final outcome of a person's life by looking at only a short period of time. We want to avoid all the mistakes and transgressions that we possibly can, but we must also realize the fact that people can change!

2. *Growth Toward Perfection* (Ten Years)

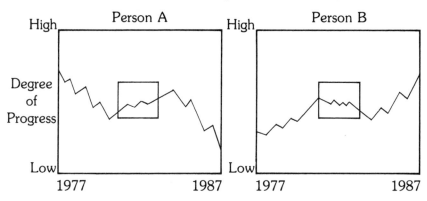

One of the great stories in the scriptures recounts the life of a young man who had been taught the truth, but rejected it. Alma rebelled against the truth to such an extent that he and his friends, the sons of King Mosiah, were described as "the very vilest of sinners" (Mosiah 28:4). Alma himself was referred to as a "very wicked and an idolatrous man," who led others to follow his iniquitous ways, even to the point of trying to destroy the Church (Mosiah 27:8-10).

Alma experienced a remarkable conversion which resulted in a complete change in attitude, beliefs, and behavior. Through proper repentance, he and his four friends became great missionaries and leaders in the Church. Alma later received the highest religious calling (high priest over the church) and governmental position (chief judge over all the land) that he could receive—evidence of his thorough and complete change.

I once had a rebellious ninth-grade seminary student respond to my encouragement to make a turnaround in his life by saying:

41

"If I had an angel appear to me and show me a vision of hell, like Alma did, I'd change too!" Many of us think a heavenly manifestation would change our attitudes and behavior, but experience has shown that does not always happen. In fact, two other rebellious characters in the Book of Mormon, Laman and Lemuel, had numerous miraculous "encouragements" to turn around, but their change of heart was only temporary.

I believe the important message of Alma's experience is not the circumstances that led to his repentance, but the fact that he *could* change. He made a conscious choice regarding his future; and he was willing to make the adjustments in his lifestyle, even at the risk of ridicule. It was a total change!

Why Not Just Once?

Another misconception associated with conversion stories, ancient and modern, is the notion that one who rebels and later repents is better off than one who remains faithful always. There is a lot of attention given to those who return to the fold. After all, aren't they much wiser, having learned by their own experience of the advantages to living the gospel of Jesus Christ?

I want to conclude this chapter by reaffirming: Yes, we can be forgiven. Yes, we do rejoice over the return of the prodigal. Yes, we can gain valuable experience from our mistakes. *However,* I still believe it is infinitely better to obey God's commandments and stay in the fold, than it is to have to repent. Here are just a few of my reasons:

1. To purposely rebel with the intention of repenting later is a form of mockery toward God and the Savior. I believe that such an attitude requires repentance as much as the acts of rebellion themselves.

2. We lose the strength and integrity that result from being able to say, "I never have." What power a father has when he is able to respond appropriately to a teenage son's blunt questions, "Dad, did you ever go inactive in the Church?" or "Dad, did you ever steal?" or "Dad, did you ever commit fornication?"

3. We may observe the penitent soul return to activity and a happy life, but be unaware of the untold others who do not "come to themselves." We cannot know whether our temporary side trip into the ways of the world may become permanent as we lose all will to repent. For every one that returns, many never do. Sin can be awfully addicting.

4. It is often difficult to repair the damage done during a period of rebelliousness. We may be forgiven, but we cannot necessarily restore to a better state all wrongs done. This was a chief concern of Alma and the sons of Mosiah as they went about "zealously striving to repair all the injuries which they had done" (Mosiah 27:35). We can never be sure whether our momentary lapses in behavior will cause eternal heartbreak in the lives of others who may have followed our negative example.

5. The time spent in transgression is time lost forever to more worthwhile pursuits. The critical years of preparing for life can never be retrieved. The development of talents, educational pursuits, and opportunities for service are often neglected during the only time available for such experiences. I recall a story about a man who got physically ill every time he saw a certain 1949 automobile, because it reminded him that in his youth he passed up an opportunity to serve a mission in order to purchase a similar vehicle.

6. A repentant sinner must live with his memories (at least throughout earth life). Memories can bring joy and gladness or they can bring stabs of pain and regret. As a teenager, I recall being extremely rude to a young lady. Since that time, I think I have never been purposely rude to another person in that manner. But I still occasionally think of that experience and feel a bit of discomfort. I wish I could apologize, but I have since lost any contact with the person. I trust it will be completely erased from my memory in eternity.

7. Finally, Lowell Bennion reminds us that all people are sinners. The only perfect life was that of Jesus Christ. "Did his life suffer from it's strength and purity?" (*New Era*, Apr. 1972, p. 9.)

It can be confidently stated that our lives will be happier and more productive to the degree that we can avoid sin altogether. Of course, we all fail to some degree in that objective, but let us not be misled into thinking sin can be good for us. We will have enough personal weaknesses to deal with by our very nature, without consciously choosing to experience the evils of life and hoping to repent later. "Wickedness never was happiness" (Alma 41:10).

5

The Case for Chastity

Jeff described himself as a confirmed agnostic when Elder Tracy and Elder Buhler first met him while walking across the university campus. His initial attitude toward the Church was strictly one of intellectual curiosity, but the enthusiasm and friendliness of the missionaries kept him interested long enough to begin reading the Book of Mormon. The witness of the Spirit prompted more serious study, so that a year later Jeff found himself sitting across the desk from the bishop being interviewed for a full-time mission.

Following the formal portion of the interview, the bishop sat back in the chair and said, "You're a rare young man! It's not often that I interview a convert to the Church who has kept himself free from sexual transgression. Yet you have done just that despite the fact that you admit to having no belief in God or life after death until you accepted the gospel. How did you manage that with all the enticements available to young people today?"

Jeff thoughtfully pondered the bishop's question before replying. "Bishop, I suppose the negative example of some members of my family convinced me that sex ought to be reserved for marriage. As you know, we didn't have any religious training in our home. Until I joined the Church, I failed to see the connection between our lack of religious training and the problems of my older brother and sisters. My brother has been married and divorced twice, and in both instances he started out the relationship by living with the girl before they were married. I have one sister who is still all mixed up emotionally from an abortion she had when she was in high school, and another sister who is desperately waiting for some medical breakthrough to provide a cure for the venereal disease she contracted from one of her boyfriends. I'd have to be stupid to ignore the consequences of their free living.

"Even though I gave little thought to the religious reasons for being morally clean, as I observed people and thought about what makes them happy and what makes them miserable, free sex just didn't seem to make sense. Now that I understand the gospel plan for mankind, it all fits into place. But even before my conversion I was convinced that I would wait until marriage, and I am so glad that I did."

Jeff is an exceptional individual, but the fact remains that there are many like him who choose to be morally clean for reasons other than belief in God or an afterlife. You need to know that chastity makes sense, regardless of one's religious beliefs. In the pages that follow I will share some reasons why those who care deeply about mental health, physical health, happy people, strong families, pleasant communities, strong nations, and the future of our civilization, will also care deeply about chastity.

The Interpersonal Effects of Unchastity

What effect does petting, fornication, or adultery have on the development of the relationship between two people who care about each other? We live in a time when society seems to be down-playing the importance of the traditional moral code of pre-marital chastity, but at the same time stressing the importance of quality interpersonal relationships and positive feelings between people.

I want to stress two reasons for living the law of chastity that relate directly to the quality of interpersonal relationships. Your

46

ability to develop a relationship with another will be a major deter-
minant of your future happiness. It is my firm conviction that premarital sex experiences will seriously hamper any relationship—
sooner or later.

1. *Premarital sex leads to a misunderstanding of the role of the
physical aspect of a relationship.*

Todd and Shellie

I purposely avoided her at school and haven't called for nearly a
week. Shellie and I had been dating regularly for nearly three
months. I really liked her and knew that she liked me—especially the
way things developed the last month or so. But last week, we got a
little carried away, and I'm just not sure of anything anymore. Sure, it
was exciting, and she seemed just as anxious as I was. So why am I
going to such great lengths to avoid her? I'll have to admit that I don't
feel very proud of the way I took advantage of her affection for me,
but I just don't feel the same about her anymore. I'm not blaming her.
She probably feels the same about me.

Sex is one of the most powerful interpersonal experiences two
people can have. A couple introduced to this physical aspect of a
relationship too soon usually finds that the continuance of the
relationship becomes almost totally dependent on gratifying the
sexual attraction. Because their thoughts and activities together
center on sex, other aspects of the relationship suffer. Such imma-
ture couples fail to develop an enduring companionship based on
social, emotional, spiritual, and personality factors, as well as the
physical.

Even when the couple marries, the emphasis on sexual gratification before marriage may result in unreal expectations after
marriage. The couple is often disappointed to find that marriage is
more than being "turned on" every time they are together. Once
the vows of marriage allow the couple to enjoy physical intimacy as
frequently as they both desire, the sexual tension tends to diminish.
Unless other reasons exist to keep the marriage alive and growing,
disenchantment often sets in and one or both find the secretary at
the office or the talk show personality much more exciting than the

spouse. Disenchantment is a general dissatisfaction with marriage in general and the spouse in particular. Can you think of anything more depressing? The marriage may endure, but the relationship is dying. Marriage is friendship, companionship, communication, shared activities, solving problems, reaching goals—as well as physical intimacy.

As I occasionally chat with engaged and dating couples, I find a common concern: "How can we be sure we can have a loving relationship that will endure?" I try to impress them with the importance of holding their physical affection in check, so that the compatability of their personalities and interests can be tested during the courtship. When couples let their physical desires dictate, there seems to be a nagging fear that they are not really as compatible as they suspect. The only truly confident couples are those who, early in courtship, begin to build an eternal relationship that is not dominated by lust or physical gratification. Many young people are swept swiftly along through courtship, engagement, wedding ceremony, and the physical excitement of the honeymoon only to awaken a few weeks into marriage to the fact that they don't really know each other.

In marriage, the same selfishness that led to immorality before marriage tends to surface, with both partners manipulating, exploiting, and using each other as things—not just physically, but in other ways as well. They have not learned to relate on the more intimate emotional and spiritual levels because of the pattern set in courtship.

2. *Premarital sex leads to a profound loss of trust and security.*

Ken and Lisa

Every time we have an argument, Lisa cries and then brings up the old problem. She's never been able to get over the fact that we were not exactly worthy when we were married seven years ago. But we were just kids then. We didn't realize what we were doing.

Last night, she accused me of purposely staying late at the office just to avoid coming home. To be honest, its no real thrill to be around Lisa anymore. When we were dating, our relationship was great, but since we've been married, it's been downhill all the way. I don't think she's ever forgiven herself for not marrying in the temple. And now, I'm not sure we could ever care enough for each other to want to be together for eternity.

Vital to any worthwhile relationship is trust. Trust has been defined as "firm reliance on the integrity, ability, or character of a person." It involves knowing that another will act in a caring and responsible manner toward you. It has been said that to be trusted is better than to be loved; and in a marriage relationship, being able to trust and be trusted is one of the foundation stones upon which enduring love is built.

Premarital or extramarital sex will do more to sow seeds of mistrust and doubt than almost any other act. This is especially true among those who share a value system in which chastity is a highly cherished virtue. But even among the worldly nothing tends to cause lying, deceit, and associated loss of integrity as much as infidelity.

Let's do an object lesson. Suppose you and I are together, and I ask you to stand stiff and fall backward into my arms. You are to trust me. I will not let you fall on the floor. The first time you do this, depending on your size, you will probably be a bit uneasy, not knowing for sure if I am strong enough to catch you. Possibly you are afraid I might be deceiving you, intending to get a good laugh as you crash painfully onto the hard floor. However, as I am successful in catching you, not just once, but many times, you relax; for now your trust in me is based on experience. If, for some reason, we continued to do this every day for two years, you would come to rely totally on me, having no reason to mistrust my ability or motives.

On one occasion, after hundreds of successful catches, I quickly jump to one side and laugh heartily as your body meets the floor. As you slowly pick yourself up with a look of hurt and betrayal in your eyes, I apologize and tell you that I really didn't mean anything. I just got bored and wanted to see what it was like to let you fall for once. I promise never to do it again.

The next day, as we prepare to perform our daily ritual, how are you going to feel? Will you stand confident and erect and fall safely into my arms as you had for the previous two years (except for yesterday)? Or will you be a little bit hesitant? Maybe a little distrustful? Even if I convince you that I will behave, how many times will we have to repeat our exercise before you will be as trusting as you were before my betrayal? Don't you see that it will take me much longer to regain your confidence the second time than it took initially? In fact, I may never fully regain your trust, for you may always remember the pain you felt as your head hit the floor, because I wanted a little fun. You may always have a nagging doubt that I might do it again.

When we desire to develop a relationship with someone we love that will last for this life and on into eternity, we should do everything within our power to establish trust. Avoid or eliminate anything from your character or relationship that would diminish trust. I am saying to you that premarital and extramarital indiscretions will prevent you from building the kind of marriage relationship you will need. Steve Gilliland writes of the doubt that creeps into the relationship for both parties when premarital sex standards are violated: "Does he love me for what I am or just for the pleasure he receives?" "If he loves me, why doesn't he respect my standards?" "Did she marry me because she loves me, or because she feels that no one else will have her?" "He says that I'm the only one, but is there someone else?" "Is she comparing me with someone else?" (See *Ensign*, July 1975, p. 55.)

Do you know friends who after breaking the moral code to one degree or another no longer felt comfortable around each other? In fact, it is not uncommon for one to actually despise or hate the other, often within hours or days of the loss of chastity. Do you remember Todd's feelings toward Shellie in the case study earlier in this chapter?

I recall the biblical story of Amnon and the beautiful Tamar. Amnon is described as being so much in love with Tamar that he became ill just thinking about her. His friend, Jonadab, suggested a subtle plan to enable Amnon to be alone with Tamar. When they were finally together, "he took hold of her, and said unto her, Come lie with me" (2 Samuel 13:11).

Tamar tried to talk sense to Amnon, expressing a willingness to marry him, but "he would not hearken unto her voice: but, being stronger than she, forced her, and lay with her" (2 Samuel 13:14).

The next verse describes the effect the premarital experience had on Amnon: "Then Amnon *hated her exceedingly;* so that the hatred wherewith he hated her was greater than the love wherewith he had loved her. And Amnon said unto her, Arise, be gone." (2 Samuel 13:15; emphasis added.)

How many times in history has a potential loving relationship turned to ashes by the inability of one or both to exercise self-control over the physical desires?

Many social scientists have been able to link premarital chastity with healthy adjustment to marriage and positive relationships with others. It is interesting to know that the conclusions of many researchers often confirm our own beliefs and feelings, but often your own observations can be as accurate. What has been your own experience, and the experience of those close to you? Don't be fooled by those who tend to justify their own immorality. If you are observant, you can see through the cockiness of the girl who boasts of her "meaningful relationship," or the macho guy who finds security only in bragging or while under the influence of alcohol or other stimulant that props up his ego and hides the insecurities felt deep within.

Confidence, security, and trust result from a relationship built on honor and integrity. Many today who have lost the perspective of chastity as a desirable virtue nevertheless see the importance of proper concern about relationships and inner peace. It is not just sexual abstinence or fidelity that results in a truly moral person, but the totality of thought, action, desire, and intent in our relationships with others. Remember that it is possible to be technically chaste and yet still be unfaithful to another.

The Psychological Case for Chastity

Because physical intimacy is such a powerful psychological experience, it must be surrounded with proper precautions and preparation. Many suffer negative consequences from premature experiences or stimuli, as illustrated in this excerpt from a brief autobiography of a college-aged young woman engaged to be married:

> I had bad experiences in school; everyone does. But I had an especially traumatic experience in the third grade. One day Alan followed me home from school. My mother worked and my brother and sister didn't come home for quite a while after me, so I was the only one at home. Alan knocked on my door and I answered it. He was direct and to the point. He wanted to come in and kiss me. I was so horrified with the idea I slammed the door and locked it. By this time my heart was beating ninety miles a minute and I was terrified beyond belief. Now this may sound quite trivial, but I assure you that to a little girl it is a frightening experience. I was so scared that I hid under the kitchen table and cried. This whole time he was pounding on the door wanting in. Our neighbor came and rescued me and all was well except for the fact that when the rest of my friends were having crushes through grade school and junior high, I couldn't stand to have a male any closer than three feet from me, and heaven forbid should one try to touch me. That experience left a scar that took years to heal. Even when I was older and dating I didn't want to be touched. I've overcome this now; and now when I think of it, I'd like to beat that little brat in the brain a couple of times and see how well that might set with him.

Traditionally, families and society structured relationships between the sexes so that young people were given sufficient time to mature physically, emotionally, and socially before having to deal with sex. Today, however, it is not uncommon for grade school children to experiment with kissing or petting, or at least be exposed to sexual stimuli via television, magazine pictures, or the movies. We need to consider the heavy psychological burden we are placing on youth who grow up too soon.

A sixteen-year-old girl wrote the following letter to Ann Landers:

Dear Ann Landers:

I will be a senior in high school and so will my boyfriend. We have been going together for about 2½ years. I guess by now it is love. We broke up a few times, but we always got back together. Now I have a serious problem.

We started to have sex six months after we began to go steady. I held off as long as I could. At first it was very exciting, but the excitement is gone and I don't feel like making love nearly as much as I used to — if at all. I only wish to heaven I had never started in with this sex thing. After we are through, I am really turned off and I want him to leave me alone. I know this sounds childish, but I can't explain my feelings because I am so mixed up and ashamed of myself. Thank God no one knows! Can you give me some advice? — Desperate at 16. (*Idaho Statesman*, 30 Aug. 1980.)

At a time when a young lady ought to be enjoying life to the fullest with school, hobbies, dates, and family relationships, "Desperate at 16" is burdened with mental confusion. Do the following excerpts from the letter tell you something? "The excitement is gone." "I wish I had never started with this sex thing." "I am really turned off." "I want him to leave me alone." "I can't explain my feelings." "I am so mixed up and ashamed of myself." Guilt feelings, emotional imbalance, lack of self-understanding, poor self-esteem, disenchantment with sex, a feeling of despair — these are often the psychological effects of premarital intimacy. It's really not a very pleasant situation for one so young. It is also obvious that this young lady is not burdened by religious prohibitions; in fact, she concludes her letter by thanking God that no one knows.

The above case study is so common today that one wonders how the popular press can continue to paint a picture of freedom, self-discovery, and happiness as the fruits of the new morality. The truth of the matter is that right-thinking people do recognize the potential problems of unchastity, but their voices are being drowned out by those who are seeking to become popular or wealthy at the expense of others, or by those who are willfully perverse. Such false voices care not for the development of the whole man or the good of society, but they themselves have succumbed to the great physical lie — that happiness is in physical things, physical appearances, and physical pleasures. In order to maintain some sense of integrity in the face of their own lack of self control, these so-called experts delight in justifying sexual freedom in the name of science or progress.

The Historical-Social Case for Chastity

Many of you who will read this book were born since 1960 — just about the time the "sexual revolution" got up a good head of steam. You have never known a world where sexual stimuli weren't ever-present (as they are today). If you could somehow board a time machine and take a quick trip back to the beginning of recorded history, and quickly get a bird's-eye view of what it would have been like to live in past periods of time, what would you learn? What would 6,000 years of historical perspective teach you about the effects of chastity (or unchastity) on humankind? What would you observe in Athens during the golden era of Greece? What would you find in ancient Assyria, Sodom and Gomorrah, or the mighty Roman Empire that would help us live happier today? Do you think we could learn from the Dark Ages, the Nephites following the visit of Christ, Italy during the Renaissance, or Colonial America? Would there be some consistent patterns in the sexual practices of the people and the happiness and progress of the society?

Many great historians have concluded that nearly every civilization has collapsed from moral decay *within* the society! I remember hearing an interesting statement once: "A savage takes a lifetime to learn what it took his father a lifetime to learn." Could it be that those societies that do not study and learn from the past are condemned to repeat their mistakes? I am convinced from my own study of history that chastity is essential for the very survival of our nation.

Actually, the fruits of chastity or unchastity are so evident today that we really do not even need the perspective of the time machine to determine the best way to live. Jeff was wise enough to see the immediate effects of immorality on his own family, friends, and society. Look around you. Read the newspaper. Watch the news. Has modern man risen to new heights of happiness and joy as a result of our permissive society?

While sitting in an introductory college class, Chris was irritated by the condescending attitude the instructor seemed to have toward religion in general and religious moral standards in particular. The young professor seemed to take great delight in cracking jokes about virginity and other "old-fashioned" attitudes toward sex. Fearing ridicule from the instructor and others in the class, Chris remained silent. However, he wanted very much to have an opportunity to speak up. His chance to present his views in a proper context came when the class was assigned a term paper on a topic of their own choosing, to be presented orally to the entire class.

Chris feverishly searched the library for sources describing the negative effects of sexual permissiveness. Never had Chris worked so intently on a school assignment, and his diligence was rewarded with page after page of documented material describing health problems, family breakdown, venereal disease, abortion, welfare costs to the taxpayers, and so on, all related directly or indirectly to sexual permissiveness. He included the views of several historians describing the decline and fall of past civilizations. He felt that his evidence would withstand the scrutiny of the professor and his classmates. Chris finally polished his sentence structure and wording by writing and rewriting, so that his ideas were clear and understandable.

Nervous, but convinced of the soundness of his argument, Chris presented his paper. When he finished there was a brief moment of silence. First the instructor, and then the entire class, stood and vigorously applauded his presentation. Later, his instructor privately expressed his admiration for the thoroughness and objectivity of Chris's research, and apologized for using his position as instructor to be humorous at the expense of Chris's strongly held beliefs.

Whether or not you put forth a similar academic effort, you can be assured that the Lord's command, "Be ye clean" (D&C 38:42), is based on more than just eternal logic that will become evident only after you and I pass on into the eternities. The commandments are given by a wise Father who knows exactly what will lead to happiness and growth in *this* life, as well as in the existence to follow mortality.

You need never be at a loss for an explanation to those who question your standards of purity. The wisdom of the ages and the evidence of those all around us confirm the crucial importance of chastity. But isn't it great to know that by listening to our loving Father, by following his counsel through the prophets, the scriptures, and the inspiration of the Holy Ghost, we can avoid the hazards and stumbling blocks of this life, even if we aren't all historians or social scientists?

6

A Look at Love

When Marvin Payne pondered writing a book about love, he first thought: "No, it's too fine for the kind of words I could write." I am glad, though, that he chose to put his feelings into the written word, for he has succeeded in helping us grasp some extremely intangible ideas. I recommend *The Love Book* (Bookcraft, 1980) to you. In it, Marvin Payne writes of rosebuds and trees and oranges and ashes and love. Likewise, I trust that the words I use will enhance rather than detract from your understanding of love.

What Is Love?

When I was about fifteen years old, we listened to a popular song by the Playmates entitled "What Is Love?" Their answer was "five feet of heaven in a pony-tail." Now that may not be the most poetic or profound definition of love, but it apparently struck a responsive chord in the hearts of America's teenagers in the late fifties.

The top-forty song charts of today continue to be filled with songs about "love." Unfortunately, most popular music, movies, and literature glorify cheap imitations of love—but not the real thing. How would *you* recognize love if you saw it? Do you know what to look for? How should you feel if you are truly in love? I know you understand that there are different kinds of love, such as love of God for man, love between friends, and love for humanity, as well as romantic love between a man and a woman. What you may not understand is how to know when you are experiencing the kind of romantic love that is the kind that can last for eternity. It is very difficult to interpret our feelings toward the opposite sex, and our modern society doesn't make it any easier. For example, passion, sentimentality, emotionalism, pity, physical pleasure, and raw lust have all been mistakenly labeled "love" by those who do not understand what it really is. The entertainment media, of course, simply want to make a dollar at the expense of the public, and give little regard to what they are portraying in the books, movies, and songs of today. Most people like to pride themselves on recognizing genuine love, but unfortunately most settle for a cheap substitute. Why are so many fooled by love's counterfeits?

President Kimball accurately labeled what many today are actually feeling. While counseling a young couple who had repeatedly violated the sexual code, but justified their actions because they "loved" each other, he countered firmly: "No, my beloved young people, you did not *love* each other. Rather, you *lusted* for each other." (*Love vs. Lust,* BYU Publications, 1965, p. 5.) The word *lust* has such a negative, selfish, low sound to it, that most refuse to admit that lust has a place in their feelings toward another. Nevertheless, when the satisfaction of bodily urges takes precedence over all other considerations, there is no other term to describe the behavior. Certainly the last word that ought to be used is love, for it is the exact opposite of lust!

The following excerpt from a letter written by a young lady to her boyfriend illustrates this point:

Dear Jim,

Last night you pleaded with me, so ardently and urgently, to "prove my love for you." You were very persuasive, and because I always want to please you and do what you want me to do, it was hard to deny you.

Today I am thankful from the bottom of a frightened and full heart that I did not let you persuade me. If I had agreed to your insistence, I would now be despising myself and hating and blaming you.

I have hardly slept during the night, but I have thought a lot. I kept thinking what a shining and beautiful word the word *purity* is. Today I do not believe that I could bear the despair and self-disgust that I would have felt if I had given in to you. . . .

Jim, I know that I will always think a lot of you, but now I feel that I cannot safely trust in you. Last night you were trying to destroy my purity and self-respect and chance of true future happiness for a few minutes of excitement and pleasure for yourself. Your talk of my proving my love for you was a bitter mockery. You proved that you do not love me. You love only yourself.

Elizabeth

(Improvement Era, Sept. 1970, p. 51.)

What is a good lover like? Erich Fromm speaks of love as primarily *giving,* not receiving (see *The Art of Loving* [New York: Bantam Books, 1956], p. 20). The ability to love as an act of giving relates to character development. A loving person has overcome his selfishness, dependency, or desire to exploit others, and has gained faith in his own human powers. Some are taught how to love in the family setting, and it seems to come naturally to them later in life. Others struggle to learn the art as adults—and succeed! Whether the ability to love is innate, learned as a child, or developed as an adult, it is the most powerful striving in man. Fromm describes love as "the force which keeps the human race together. . . . The failure to achieve it means insanity or destruction—self-destruction or the destruction of others. Without love, humanity could not exist for a day." (*The Art of Loving,* p. 15.)

The practice of love requires great self-discipline, concentration, patience, and supreme concern for another. It is an act of faith—both in oneself and in the potential of others. The practice of love requires the development of the best in oneself and in others. A good synonym for love is "caring;" but the best description of a truly loving person that I have found was revealed by God to Paul and to Mormon in 1 Corinthians 13 and Moroni 7.

Sex and Love

If we truly care about another in a romantic sense, that love cannot be fully expressed unless the couple is married. Melvin Anchell writes that "marriage provides the symbol that each considers the other's happiness and welfare the most important thing in the world" (*Sex and Sanity* [New York: Macmillan Co., 1971], p. 290). If that is true, a marriage contract ought to be one tangible sign of the depth of commitment each partner has to the welfare of the other. Expressions of physical affection—a kiss, a hug, or sexual relations, must be consistent with the total relationship. Physical affection sought as an end in and of itself frustrates the development of genuine love between a couple. Marvin Payne writes that friendship can blossom into romantic love, and if nurtured and protected, romantic love can blossom into something even greater than itself—family love! (See *The Love Book,* p. 14.) A person would be foolish to deny himself the opportunity to experience the mature love that he has available to him by prematurely using the powers meant for married love. Premature sexual experience does not allow love to blossom, but rather it causes it to wilt.

Why then do so many equate sex with love? I suppose one reason is that despite our sophistication in many areas, many still do not know the difference between the two. Not having experienced the fruits of genuine love, they seem satisfied with momentary substitutes. In an excerpt from a book entitled *Interview with Sex* as published in the *Reader's Digest* we find these questions directed to the personified Sex:

Q. *Well, if love and Sex are different, why do people so often say they are "making love" when what they mean is that they are "having sex"?*

A. Partly, I suppose, because they are honestly confused. Love and Sex so often appear together that people quite naturally mistake one for the other. The truth is that Sex is a biological need triggered by hormones secreted by the glands. The person who is merely sexually aroused is concerned only with his or her own satisfaction. Once satisfied, he may not even want to be with his sexual partner. At it's crudest, you see, Sex is not particularly choosy.

Love, on the other hand, is very choosy. It insists on one particular person and no other. Sex is a passionate interest in another body. Love may be just as passionate, but its interest is in the whole personality. You can force another person to have sex with you, but you cannot force that person to love you.

Q. *I can see that love and Sex are different, but how do I know if what I feel is sexual desire or if it is really love?*

A. There is no easy answer. One way to tell is by time. There is a sort of rhythm involved in Sex — an ebb and flow. The urge builds up, and then, after physical release, it is satisfied and desire fades away.

Love, however, is different. Love is a deep and constant feeling for another person. Time has no importance. The most remarkable thing is that the other person's happiness becomes at least as important as your own. A person who loves you wants you to be happy forever.

Q. *You mentioned earlier that you are unhappy over the way Sex is being written and talked about.*

A. Yes, I've always thought of myself as pretty basic — and basically honest. Now, suddenly, I seem to have an army of self-appointed press agents who haven't the slightest hesitation about claiming virtues for me that I just don't possess and making promises in my name on which I absolutely can't deliver. Sex isn't just Sex anymore. Suddenly it's freedom, self-expression, fulfillment. My name has been turned into an adjective: sex-y. Buildings, books, cars, even foods, are sexy. The word has come to mean something better than good, stronger than truth, more desirable than value.

Q. *Apart from your own personal annoyance, though, does it really do any harm?*

A. Sure, it does harm. It sends people scooting around after false goals. It sets people up for disillusionment — like passing out maps to a phony treasure. It distracts people from finding something to live for and hope for. Worst of all, it robs young people of their birthright and mission. (Allan M. Kaufman, "Sex Speaks Out," *Reader's Digest,* Apr. 1972, pp. 227-28.)

Sex and love are different; and yet under the proper circumstances they come together as a beautiful fulfillment of two of life's major purposes: to have joy through the creation of an eternal family unit, and as an expression of genuine love between a man and a woman. Read carefully the following quote by Parley P. Pratt:

> Some persons have supposed that our natural affections were the result of a fallen and corrupt nature, and that they are *"carnal, sensual,* and *devilish,"* and therefore ought to be resisted, subdued, or overcome as so many evils which prevent our perfection, or progress in the spiritual life. In short, that they should be greatly subdued in this world, and in the world to come entirely done away. . . .
>
> Such persons have mistaken the source and fountain of happiness altogether. They have not one correct idea of the nature of the enjoyments, or happiness of heaven, or earth; of this life or any other. . . .
>
> Our natural affections are planted in us by the Spirit of God, for a wise purpose; and they are the very main-springs of life and happiness — they are the cement of all virtuous and heavenly society — they are the essence of charity, or love; and therefore never fail, but endure forever.
>
> There is not a more pure and holy principle in existence than the affection which glows in the bosom of a virtuous man for his companion. (Parley P. Pratt, quoted in *Achieving a Successful Marriage* [Church Educational System, 1976], p. 159.)

Picture a pendulum swinging toward the two extremes. On one hand, we find those who abuse the sexual powers — who consider it a natural instinct to be gratified with no regard for divine purposes, human feelings, or propriety. On the other extreme, we find those who consider sex an unpleasant necessity at best, to be tolerated only to enable mankind to perpetuate itself. In fact, some have taught that the ideal state is complete abstinence throughout life, and celibacy the highest virtue. We know that both extremes are false. Only in the center do we find the proper attitude. Sex is good, even divine — but it can be abused.

We want our natural affections toward the opposite sex to assist us in achieving a fulness of joy without letting the abuse of those affections rob us of the greatest good. It is a mistake to try to completely stifle our physical passions and deny our sexual nature. Attitudes that imply sex as something dirty, or merely to be tolerated for procreation purposes, do not reflect the fact that the sexual power is a God-given power that, properly controlled, will help us become more like our Father in Heaven.

Viktor Frankl writes of three levels of attraction of one person toward another. The most primitive level he calls *lust,* which is no more than physical stirrings caused by the bodily appearance and physical traits of another. The second and deeper level is *infatuation,* which includes emotional stirrings caused by attraction to the psychic or character traits of another personality. However, the truly mature person will relate on an even deeper level, *love,* which causes spiritual stirrings based on the permanent aspects of the other — their personality, unique traits that lie deeper than the psychic and the physical — what a person really is. (See "The Meaning of Love," in *The Case Against Pornography,* ed. David Holbrook [La Salle, Ill.: Library Press, 1973], pp. 37-38). We cannot come to love another when the physical or purely erotic traits of the other are the sole basis for attraction. Frankl goes on to add that "even in love between the sexes the body, the sexual element, is not primary; it is not an end in itself, but a means of expression. Love as such can exist without it. Where sexuality is possible, love will desire and seek it; but where renunciation is called for [such as before marriage, or during periods of separation or health problems during marriage], love will not necessarily cool or die." ("The Meaning of Love," p. 41.)

I am suggesting that the physical attraction you feel toward another can be the very motivation you need to develop a truly loving relationship — *if* you can control it. Later in marriage, these same physical desires can be a means of expressing the love you have developed, and it will be a sweet experience that will add to

63

the development of higher character traits and spirituality. Carlfred Broderick, a nationally prominent marriage counselor, said:

> I wish we did a better job in the Church of teaching people the chastity ethic without making it more difficult for them to enjoy sexual fulfillment under the proper conditions. When I interview young people for the temple, I ask, "Is there anything you want to talk about?" And they often say, "Well, we've had a hard time holding out for the temple. It's been difficult for us." And I say, "That's good. I'm glad that you're holding out, because it's really important that you keep your obligations towards God. And I'd be disappointed if it was too easy for you, because those yearnings to be close and to express yourself in those ways are holy. They are from God. It's appropriate that you should feel that way toward the person you're going to marry in a week. Now, you need to continue holding out, but I'd sure feel bad for you if you weren't having fantasies and having to plan your time so that you weren't spending too much time together. That would really be a shame." Please don't misinterpret what I say. I'm 100 percent committed to chastity, but not the fearful attitude about chastity that destroys men's or women's sexual potential. I don't think our Heavenly Father teaches that. ("A Gospel-Centered Therapy," *Dialogue*, Summer 1980, p. 72.)

How Can I Know If It's the Real Thing?

I have a son named Joseph who is nine years old—and a very loving person. He is sensitive (most of the time) to the moods and feelings of others. I recall several occasions when Joseph would sense my discouragement and give me hugs and tender kisses. My wife spent a lot of time in bed during an extended illness, and Joseph would often rub her feet with lotion and chat with her. I suspect that he will be a loving adult as well, for his attitude of caring towards others will cause people to respond in like manner to him. I hope that he will not be deceived, but will someday recognize an attitude of caring from a young lady that will result in a warm friendship, physical attraction, emotional compatibility, and eventual spiritual unity. By concentrating on the inner qualities of others, I hope he will not allow the physical to dominate. I trust his parents will have taught him sufficiently about self-control that he will be able to steer a safe course through adolescence into marriage.

Even after the marriage ceremony, it will take a lifetime to fully grow to love another unconditionally. Few newly wed couples could handle the test placed upon the marriage of Thomas Moore, the nineteenth-century poet and his lovely bride. The experience was told by Galen Drake.

My favorite love story is also a true one. Soon after he was married, Thomas Moore, the famous 19th Century Irish Poet, was called away on a business trip. Upon his return he was met at the door not by his beautiful bride, but by the family doctor.

"Your wife is upstairs," said the doctor. "But she has asked that you do not come up." And then Moore learned the terrible truth: his wife had contracted smallpox. The disease had left her once flawless skin pocked and scarred. She had taken one look at her reflection in the mirror and commanded that the shutters be drawn and that her husband never see her again. Moore would not listen. He ran upstairs and threw open the door of his wife's room. It was black as night inside. Not a sound came from the darkness. Groping along the wall, Moore felt for the gas jet.

A startled cry came from a black corner of the room. "No! Don't light the lamps!"

Moore hesitated, swayed by the pleading in the voice.

"Go!" she begged. "Please go! This is the greatest gift I can give you, now."

Moore did go. He went down to his study, where he sat up most of the night, prayerfully writing. Not a poem this time, but a song. He had never written a song before, but now he found it more natural to his mood than simple poetry. He not only wrote the words, he wrote the music too. And the next morning as soon as the sun was up, he returned to his wife's room.

He felt his way to a chair and sat down. "Are you awake?" he asked.

"I am," came a voice from the far side of the room. "But you must not ask to see me. You must not press me, Thomas."

"I will sing to you, then," he answered. And so for the first time, Thomas Moore sang to his wife the song that still lives today:

Believe me, if all those endearing young charms,
Which I gaze on so fondly today,
Were to change by tomorrow and flee in my arms,
Like fairy gifts fading away,
Thou wouldst still be adored, as this moment thou art—
Let thy loveliness fade as it will.

Moore heard a movement from the dark corner where his wife lay in her loneliness, waiting. He continued,

Let thy loveliness fade as it will,
And around the dear ruin each wish of my heart
Would entwine itself verdantly still—

The song ended. As his voice trailed off on the last note, Moore heard his bride rise. She crossed the room to the window, reached up and slowly drew open the shutters.

Poor health, disfigurement, financial reversals, and other unexpected occurrences need not weaken a marriage. A relationship built on the foundation of genuine love and nurtured through the years—boyfriend and girlfriend, husband and wife, mom and dad, grandpa and grandma—will actually be strengthened by the same experiences that often destroy others. In old age, a lifetime of sharing will culminate in a oneness that extends even beyond the grave. Dr. Lindsay R. Curtis has given us an intimate view of the love that developed between his aged parents:

The night was cold, damp, and foreboding in every sense of the word. It was the kind of night that a physician ordinarily would want to forget, yet it was a night I shall never forget!

At age ninety-four my father had lived a useful and successful life as the loving, tender, and considerate husband of his childhood sweetheart and as the overindulgent father of ten devoted children. Three months previously he had suffered a stroke that deprived him of the use of his legs and temporarily halted his speech.

Although the strength in his legs seemed gone forever, he gradually regained a partial, halting ability to talk. Despite his advanced age, all his numerous progeny had hoped and prayed for restoration of his health.

As the only member of the medical profession within our sizable family, I had brought him a considerable distance from his home town to the hospital in which I practiced so that I could be near him and watch over him with greater care. However, it now became apparent that our dad would never return to his home again. After three months of tender nursing, his once vigorous body told us that it was incapable of mending itself. It had earned the right to be laid to rest.

In the middle of the night Dad's pulse weakened to almost imperceptibility. His temperature dropped below normal. His blood pressure faltered and slowly fell. Reflexes denoted the ebbing of life as they disappeared one by one. After three months of desperate fighting, his body was no longer able to respond. Our dad was dying.

My first thought was that I should not bother my mother, whose state of health at best was precarious. She should not have her rest interrupted nor should she be brought out into the cold night on a forty-mile journey when she might be too late anyway. And if she did arrive before my father died, she would only find him in a coma.

Then it occurred to me that sixty-six years of married life together had earned each of them the right to be together at the last moment of life on this earth. Surely this was a sacred right more important than any earthly reasoning I might entertain. Neither Mother nor Dad would forgive me should I deny them this privilege.

Only with great effort did Mother make the journey to the hospital. In tender haste attendants wheeled her to the bedside of her dying companion. As was her custom when something was important, she had to stand up! She was literally lifted out of the wheelchair and onto her feet. Unsteadily she leaned over the blanched face of Dad, tenderly stroking the few gray hairs on his head.

Dad's last years had been saddened by a gradual loss of hearing, but he always heard my mother when she spoke to him! There were no tears, no sobbing by mother. She merely leaned over his head, kissed him softly, then spoke directly into his ear, "Oh, Father, I love you!"

Then something wonderful happened to this dying man. Suddenly, yet slowly, a tear welled up in the corner of his eye. Even as the tear rolled down his cheek, his pulse quickened. His blood pressure began to rise and his reflexes slowly returned. Almost undetectable at first, but finally undeniably, Father began to rouse from his coma.

We left the room, except for Mother.

When we returned, Father had lapsed back into his coma. But Mother said, "We had the grandest visit about some very important things."

You don't have to be a physician to know that the only thing on earth powerful enough to bridge the gulf between life and death is love! (Lindsay R. Curtis, "The Power of Love," *Listen*, Aug. 1968, p. 3.)

Most people today are too impatient to allow time for the proper development of love. Our nearly 50 percent divorce rate makes it obvious that many people plant, water, and nurture their love for a time, but when the excitement of courtship and beginning life together settles into the realities and challenges of family life, many abandon each other before the time of harvest. Carol Lynn Pearson wrote a few lines that remind us not to be too hasty in judging a marriage relationship:

Spring Is Only for Beginnings

Our love
Was a blossom,
Full and faultless
On the tree.
But when the petals
Began to fall,
All you could see
Were the sad
Leaves scattered
On the ground.

You did not
Think to watch
For Autumn
When the fruit
Is found.

(*New Era*, Feb. 1976, p. 50.)

Don't deny yourself the greatest fruit of mortality. Do not cheat yourself of the awesome power of human love by settling for a cheap substitute. Yes, there is a physical thrill or pleasure that accompanies the satisfaction of your sexual desires, but it pales in significance when compared with the joy of experiencing those physical affections in the proper setting of a loving marriage relationship. Consider these lines from Shakespeare's *Lucrece:*

> What win I, if I gain the thing I seek?
> A dream, a breath, a froth of fleeting joy?
> Who buys a minute's mirth to wail a week?
> Or sells eternity to get a toy?
> For one sweet grape who will the vine destroy?

We might ask today, "Who would burn down a house to roast a hot dog?"

7

Looking Through Our Spiritual Lenses

To a world fascinated with the quest for physical gratification, the challenge to develop spirituality seems strangely out of place. For example, a number-one hit song in America was entitled "Let's Get Physical." Can you imagine a song breaking into the top forty with the message "Let's Get Spiritual"? To the world at large, spirituality, as either a term or a concept, is not in common usage today.

However, in the Church of Jesus Christ, spirituality is discussed regularly in seminary and institute classes, Church meetings, and family home evenings. It seems to be a highly desirable characteristic. In fact, those possessing an abundance of true spirituality are esteemed very highly by the Latter-day Saints.

In this chapter I want to convince you that the spiritual consequences of our sexual behavior outweigh all other reasoning on the matter. The Apostle Paul reminds us that some things cannot be seen through worldly understanding, but are eternal and true nonetheless (see 2 Corinthians 4:18). A modern Apostle, Elder Neal A. Maxwell, writes that "there are some consequences of sexual immorality which we are simply not able to measure fully; but they are very real—though not seen" (*New Era*, June 1979, p. 37). Now I must caution you that the following ideas will make sense to you only if you are looking at them through your "spiritual lenses." Remember that the natural man cannot understand the things of the Spirit (see 1 Corinthians 2:14). Unless you read and ponder these things by the Spirit, and sincerely seek to live in harmony with that Spirit, they just might seem a bit foolish.

Why Not Sin?

I attended an Education Week lecture in which the instructor, Max Caldwell, asked and answered two very important questions. He first asked, "Why sin?"—and answered, "Because it feels good." I think you will agree that most people do not intentionally set out to hurt themselves when they break a commandment. It is simply more convenient or pleasurable for most people to sin than it is not to sin. Not sinning requires self-control and discipline. Sinning requires neither.

The question then becomes, "Why *not* sin?" Obviously there are many more who sin than who do not sin, so the majority must not be getting a satisfactory answer to that question. I suggest that you ask yourself that question and give it the sincere, honest thought it deserves. It is the kind of question that is usually not answered in a moment, or even in a few days or weeks of pondering. Rather, you will spend *years* evaluating the implications of that question as you grow in intellect, in experience, and in spiritual maturity.

Max Caldwell asked another penetrating question: "What happens when we sin?" What is happening to our spirit body when we smoke, or break the Sabbath, or cheat on a test, or pet? If we could see what was happening to our spirits when we sin, we would never repeat the sin! Just as our physical body is wounded when we are injured, because of physical laws that cannot be set aside, so also the spirit is scarred and seared by the effects of the spiritual laws we violate.

Unfortunately, spiritual wounds and scars and stunted growth are not so evident in our physically oriented society. But they are real, and if we could see, we would find it painful to view the broken condition of so many spirits originally created in the image of God.

Stop reading for a moment and consider the condition of your spirit. Look in the mirror of your mind's eye and give yourself a spiritual checkup. Be assured that when your doctor gives you a physical examination, he is only observing a small portion of the *real* you, for your body is an outer shell to house that unique individual we call you. Eventually, your body and spirit will become an inseparably connected whole; but your eternal destiny will depend on how carefully you control the influences that shape both your spirit and your physical body.

One of the major tests of life is to discipline the physical desires of your body. You probably know people who have allowed their physical appetites to completely dominate their behavior. In fact, many people are oblivious to the fact that they even *have* a spiritual nature. Those who understand the spiritual side of mankind recognize that the physical appetites *can* be controlled, and in time, the "war" between the body and the spirit can become a cooperative effort, with both contributing toward our exaltation and eternal happiness.

The following excerpt from the patriarchal blessing given to a sixteen-year-old girl illustrates the relationship between the body and the spirit:

> I would admonish you to take the proper care of your body to keep it free and pure and clean and innocent, that it may be a fit dwelling place for your spirit to inhabit throughout the countless ages of eternity. Keep yourself unspotted from the sins of the world. Your virtue is the greatest jewel that you possess. Guard it as such and when the time comes for you to present yourself to the man of your choice, you can present yourself to him as clean and pure as you were when you nestled close to your Mother's breast. And I promise you in the name of Israel's God that nothing will bring you more joy and happiness than that of a good clean honest upright life.
>
> You are blessed to be an attractive girl, and if you will live faithfully, this attractiveness will prove to be an asset to you, but if you keep not the commandments of our Heavenly Father, it will surely be a liability unto you.

Just as we care for the physical body through proper diet, grooming, exercise, and other kinds of attention, so also we must care for our spirit bodies by obedience to the commandments of God. King Benjamin taught his people that a natural (worldly) man is an enemy to God, and would remain so forever unless he subdued his physical desires for the sake of spiritual growth. This is done through yielding to the enticings of the Holy Spirit, made possible through the atonement of Christ (see Mosiah 3:19). Our spiritual and physical selves are inseparably intertwined.

If the experts of the world were to carefully analyze a human being, they would conclude that a whole man is more than just a particular combination of tissue, organs, water, and blood. Although centered in a *physical* body, we have recognized that man is also an *intellectual* being; he has a brain which enables him to carry on thought processes, to think rationally, and to enjoy a world apart from his physical existence. Likewise, we have identified an intangible part of man which we have come to call his *emotional* self. This includes his feelings and his subjective response to the physical or intellectual circumstances of life. Other scientists would argue that we must not leave out the *social* part of man; his behavior and happiness depend on his ability to relate to other people in society. Our whole man, then, in the eyes of the experts of the world, could be defined and explained in four categories:

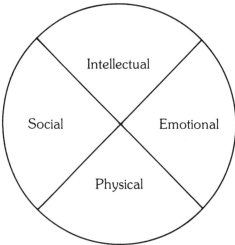

Depending on the expert you consult, he may emphasize one or another of the four categories as being the most critical to your happiness. Unfortunately, the experts often lack an essential dimension to understanding human behavior. I am speaking, of course, of our *spirit*. To truly understand a person, we must consider the effect our choices and behavior will have on our spiritual selves; then our diagram would look like this:

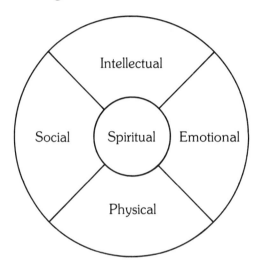

The Spiritual Blessings of Chastity

If we fully understood why the Lord insists on a pure people, we would be less likely to give in to the worldly desires associated with mortality. Too often, we consider only the negative consequences of transgression (which are very real), rather than the positive blessings and additional knowledge that come with obedience. Let me outline a hypothetical sequence of growth and blessings that one can anticipate as a result of living a chaste life.

Dan is a popular senior in high school, involved in most church activities, and one of five children in a moderately committed LDS family. He has faced most of the normal challenges associated with growing up, but has had a particularly difficult struggle with his thoughts and behavior related to moral worthiness. His bishop hasn't taken the time to interview him for a couple of years, so he has slipped into some habits that make him feel unworthy to pray, bless the sacrament, or participate in seminary. Lately, he has been wondering if he should just forget about going on a mission. Our prophet has called for more *worthy* young men and women —and he feels he would not qualify.

Deep down inside, Dan wants to change, for he does not feel good about himself. He has lost count of the times he has made promises to the Lord in prayer—only to have broken them at the first sign of temptation. Dan has concluded that he is basically a "terrestrial" person—not a bad guy, just incapable of living up to the high standards of the celestial kingdom.

If we were to examine Dan's self-esteem, we would find it to be suffering from malnutrition. He feels pretty good about himself on the basketball court or in his chemistry class, and he knows that the kids at school like to be around him. The fact remains, however, that Dan is not living up to the covenants he made at baptism, nor has he kept the promises made to the bishop when he was ordained a priest nearly two years ago. All the success in the world is not sufficient to erase the feelings that come when you are not true to yourself. Dan knew he was failing—and he knew that God knew.

Let's just suppose that Dan attends a youth conference and is highly motivated by a speaker who really seems to understand the struggles of young people. Thinking about his circumstances, he concludes to talk to his bishop. The most painful part was making the appointment. After explaining his problem, his bishop quickly put him at ease. Dan learned that his problems were not too untypical. In fact, the bishop didn't even act shocked or surprised. On the other hand, the bishop assured Dan that God could not look upon sin with the least degree of allowance, as it says in Doctrine and Covenants 1:31. The Lord would expect full and complete repentance.

Dan is at a critical turning point. He feels the great relief that comes from confession and the accompanying hope for a brighter future. However, Dan may not fully realize that the greatest test remains ahead of him.

For several days, Dan felt that nothing could ever cause him to fail in his commitments to the Lord and to the bishop. But, gradually, the resolves of that experience began to fade, while the old habits and temptations seemed to grow in strength. On one occasion, Dan crawled into bed without prayer—the first time in two weeks that he had missed. He did not forget. He felt unworthy. Again, those tormenting thoughts, "Why try? How can I ever hope to change?"

When the bishop failed to see Dan at priesthood meeting, he wisely made an appointment for another visit. On this occasion, the bishop did not scold or chastise. He lovingly explained the realities of true repentance, and restored Dan's faith in himself and in the atoning sacrifice of Jesus Christ. "Remember how you felt when you left my office last month?" the bishop inquired. "How did you feel about yourself?" Dan described the feelings of personal strength and self-esteem that resulted from doing a difficult thing that needed to be done.

"Dan, there are few feelings in life that can compare to the peace of mind that results from self-control and integrity of soul. You felt good about yourself for doing the right thing, but you mistakenly assumed that all temptation was behind you. It will take some time for your physical body to respond to the direction of your spirit. Let me encourage you to discipline your thoughts and actions for two more weeks. We will meet again two weeks from today to check on your progress."

Again, Dan left the bishop's office feeling renewed, but more aware of the difficulty of the task before him. He walked with strength and courage, finding joy in prayer, scripture study, and attendance at his meetings.

As he entered the bishop's office two weeks later, the smile on his face and the firmness of his handshake were all the bishop needed to know that Dan had kept his commitments. He asked Dan to turn to Doctrine and Covenants 121:45, and explain what words in that verse seemed especially important to him today.

Dan carefully read that familiar verse and thought of the confidence he felt in the presence of a servant of God. "Bishop, I can honestly say that for the past two weeks, virtue *has* garnished my thoughts unceasingly. I did it!"

The bishop went on to teach Dan about the remaining promises contained in that revelation. He learned of the doctrine of the priesthood. The bishop taught Dan regarding the oath and covenant of the Melchizedek Priesthood, and explained that, with continued purity, the Holy Ghost would literally become Dan's constant companion.

The months passed with occasional trials and problems, but Dan learned by experience that the Lord consoles the pure in heart in their afflictions, as it says in Jacob 3:1. He gained a greater appreciation for the love of his bishop and family and began to ponder the meaning of love in all the relationships in his life. A sacrament meeting speaker quoted a passage that seemed to leap off the page for Dan. He read in Alma 38:12: "see that ye bridle all your passions, that ye may be filled with love." It was like a revelation to him. Love and lust were opposites! Only by controlling the passions could one come to experience genuine love! For weeks, he found himself analyzing his feelings toward the girls he had been dating, and for the first time began to think seriously about preparing himself to be able to love someone in an eternal way.

As the months and years passed, Dan found himself experiencing growth he had never dreamed possible. His desire to serve a full-time mission grew steadily as his testimony of eternal principles increased. His struggle to prepare for that high calling caused him to read the scriptures for understanding and strength, and his efforts were rewarded.

Full-time missionary service opened new vistas of love for God's other children. He found himself teaching sincere investigators the plan of salvation with confidence and authority. One morning, he and his companion were reading in the New Testament together and came across the following passage in 2 Peter 1:4: "Whereby are given unto us exceeding great and precious promises: that by these ye might be partakers of the divine nature, having escaped the corruption that is in the world through lust."

Dan thought of his progress through the last four years of his life. He understood that the greatest challenges of life still lay before him — he had only begun the race. But he also felt a burning assurance from the Holy Ghost that he was on the right course.

Dan and his companion read verses five through seven where Peter outlines the step-by-step sequence of growth: faith, virtue, knowledge, temperance, patience, godliness, brotherly kindness, and charity. Dan wondered how he could have overlooked the power in those verses during the first twenty years of his life. Together, he and his companion completed reading that great chapter, recognizing the necessity of those eight qualities in their lives. They rejoiced in their assurance that Christ was their Savior, and rededicated their efforts to helping others to *see*. Peter taught that without those qualities we are blind, unable to see afar off, and forgetting what we had formerly known to be true. Dan desired with all his heart to have his calling and election made sure (see 2 Peter 1:10) by putting himself in remembrance of these things daily.

Dan cannot fully appreciate how much more joy awaits him as he continues his efforts to be pure and Christlike. He has only just begun! The greatest happiness in mortality is associated with getting married and having a family. There is also much pain associated with marriage and parenthood, but you and I both know that good things don't come free.

It's difficult to tell you exactly how it will feel when you kneel in purity across the altar of the temple with the one you love. You must experience for yourself the deep inner feelings associated with preparing for the birth of your first child. I am still experiencing the many "firsts" of being a father — watching a child perform in a school play, baptizing and confirming a daughter, ordaining a son to the priesthood. I cannot tell you how I will feel when I send my children on missions, or witness their marriages in the temple, or hold my own grandchild in my arms. Both you and I will have to experience those earthly joys for ourselves to fully appreciate them.

And after this life is over, then what? Can I suggest that the best of this life is only a taste — a sampling — of what is in store. Remember the passage "eye hath not seen, nor ear heard, neither have entered into the heart of man, the things which God hath prepared for them that love him" (1 Corinthians 2:9). Our imaginations fall short of picturing eternal doings, but the Spirit can motivate us to seek them. I don't feel capable of even trying to describe the rewards that await us beyond this life. I think you and I will each have to gain that through the Spirit. I know that sincere, careful reading of the scriptures will enable you to learn about things which no other person can teach you. Read sections 131 and 132 of the Doctrine and Covenants, and see if you don't agree that the Lord has some great things in store for those couples who can learn to love each other in an eternal way.

The Spiritual Consequences of Unchastity

After describing the blessings of chastity—high self-esteem, peace of mind, confidence before God, a sure knowledge of Christ, spiritual power, a loving spouse and children, and eternal life in the world to come—it doesn't seem necessary to write this section. However, the scriptures and the prophets have made it clear that specific spiritual consequences result from disregarding God's laws of chastity.

Dave, one of Dan's high school friends, likewise struggled with chastity, but his life took a different course. Following high school graduation, Dave attended the university, but just didn't feel very comfortable at church or the institute; so he gradually dropped into inactivity. He, too, had felt a sense of guilt and unworthiness (the first stage of alienation from God); but unlike Dan, who chose to repent and forsake his bad habits, Dave wallowed in this stage of fear and despair until he began to rationalize his behavior. He no longer felt guilty or unworthy, but sought to justify his actions as "better than most," "not that serious," or even "normal." He gradually grew desensitized to the Spirit, to the point that he was "past feeling" (see 1 Nephi 17:45).

Having turned his back on the light of the commandments, Dave's analysis of his condition is grossly inaccurate. He is ripe for falling into a state of defiant independence—abandoning any attempt to live a moral and good life. The prophet Mormon records the results of an entire nation rejecting God's standards of purity. He describes their situation as the "sorrowing of the damned" — no longer able to take pleasure in sin, but not willing or able to change (see Mormon 2:12-15). Can you think of a more miserable situation than to get no satisfaction out of sin and yet have no desire to change? We see people today who are caught up in a vicious cycle of habit and addiction. They are alienated from God, from society, from their families, and even from themselves. Alma describes such a condition as the "chains of hell" (Alma 12:11). To break out of such a condition to the realm of peace of conscience is most difficult, and certainly the greatest task before mankind. Fortunately, the spiral leading downward can also lead up.

The choice before us, though clear, is not easy. Elder Boyd K. Packer said, "The choice of life is not between fame and obscurity, nor is the choice between wealth and poverty. The choice is between good and evil." (*Ensign*, Nov. 1980, p. 21.) If we were living our lives in a cocoon, protected from the influences of those who do not share our values, it would be fairly easy to live a pure life. But, we live in a world of opposition in all things, and part of the test of life is not just to *identify* the correct choices, but *live* those choices in the midst of others who may taunt or tempt us to conform to their way of behaving. It takes most of us many years of experience to finally come to grips with that dilemma: will we serve the living God and our own conscience, or will we serve the wishes and whims of our friends and society? Possibly this statement by President Spencer W. Kimball will give you strength to live according to the right choices you have made:

> Do not be puzzled if sometime there are those in the world who mock how you live and what you believe, saying it is all false, but who, deep inside themselves, are really afraid that what you believe is really true (*New Era*, April 1980, p. 36).

You have the truth; but to be wishy-washy in your commitment to purity will leave you uncertain and unsure. Live true today and you will eventually come to know for a certainty!

8

The Spirit Is Willing, but the Flesh Is Weak

Bob and his roommate Alan talked late into the evening. "You know, Alan, I really want to be clean," Bob said, "but it's so hard for me. After I've talked to the bishop I feel strong for a while, but sooner or later I find myself fighting a war in my mind to keep my thoughts clean so I can control the desires of my body. Do you think it will always be like this? I've served a mission. I'm active in the Church. Is something wrong with me? I suppose I'm doing pretty good compared to a lot of guys, but I'm afraid that I might buckle under the pressure and do something that would jeopardize my chances for a happy life."

They talked, and Bob was strengthened. But as they concluded, his friend cautioned: "Our greatest challenges come when we are alone, with no bishop, parent, or friend to keep us strong. Just as the Savior had his Gethsemane, we must conquer our weaknesses alone, except for the influence of the Holy Spirit."

We actually have two challenges before us. First, to obtain a strong *desire* to be morally clean; and second, to act on that desire—that is, to *be* morally clean. Assuming that we have the desire, let's turn to the counsel God has given regarding *how* we can stay morally clean. In the final analysis, it will be up to each one of us to make of our lives what we will. Alma said to his son Corianton, "Therefore, O my son, whosoever *will* come may come . . . and whosoever *will not* come the same is not compelled to come" (Alma 42:27; emphasis added).

Our Commitment to Christ

Do you remember the book or movie about Dr. Jekyll and Mr. Hyde? Dr. Jekyll was a respected man of the community who at times changed into an uncontrollable maniac. An extreme case of schizophrenia, to be sure. I think all of us have a split personality to a degree. It's not easy to be reminded that we were the choicest spirits in the pre-earth life, a royal priesthood, the seed of Abraham, the elect of God, the future leaders of the kingdom, destined to become kings and queens in eternity—only to walk out of the chapel or seminary building into the harsh realities of living and being accepted in a fallen world.

Alicia found herself in that situation after attending a couple of her classes at school one afternoon. Her Family Living instructor was a very stylish and impressive young woman in her mid-twenties, well liked by all of the students. Following a film entitled *Understanding Sex*, the discussion turned to what the instructor described as a "sensible" approach to teenage sexuality. Premarital relations were viewed as a normal part of growth, masturbation was encouraged, and homosexuality was depicted as an alternate sexual option available to all. Alicia wondered how the teacher and the rest of the class could feel the way they did about practices she had always assumed to be so wrong. Yet as she listened to them she also found herself wondering if perhaps they were right.

After class, Alicia slowly walked across the street to the seminary building. She was deep in thought as she sat at her desk and randomly thumbed through her scriptures. Brother Blake's lesson was on the importance of letting Jesus Christ be the center of our lives. Normally, Alicia enjoyed seminary. But today she was deeply troubled by the conflicting standards competing for her loyalty. As Brother Blake concluded his lesson and dismissed the class, he walked over to Alicia and said, "You look like you have the weight of the world on your shoulders! Cheer up! The gospel's true!"

"Oh, is it, Brother Blake? Is it really?" she blurted out, and burst into tears with pent-up emotions overflowing. "I'm so confused. When I listen to you or my parents, or when I read the scriptures, the gospel seems so logical and true. But when I'm across the street at the school our beliefs seem so unreal, so out of touch with the kind of life everybody seems to be living and enjoying."

Brother Blake acknowledged the frustration Alicia was feeling, and assured her that her dilemma was not unusual. "In fact," he said, "most of us can be labeled 'double minded' as we try to find ourselves and our relationship to God. At times we feel strong in our commitment and ability to live gospel principles. At other times we feel confusion and weakness. We temporarily lose perspective, our desire falters, and occasionally our ability to live properly takes a nose-dive. James described the double-minded person as being like a wave of the sea, driven with the wind and tossed, and the Savior taught us the futility of trying to serve two masters." (See James 1:6-8 and Matthew 6:24.)

As Brother Blake spoke, Alicia knew that the things he was saying were true. Her mind, her heart, and her conscience all united to confirm that her standards were correct. She marveled how easily she had been deceived, and made a promise to herself to avoid the mental and spiritual apathy that could cause her to doubt the standards she knew were true.

Most people in the Church are still trying to enjoy the benefits of two worlds. Their experience and study cause them to want to live in the world of the gospel, but the bright lights and pleasures of the "large and spacious building" spoken of by Lehi and Nephi are too attractive to reject completely. The consequence is a mediocre commitment to Christ based upon temporary moods or circumstances. Sooner or later a choice must be made.

Wouldn't it be great to reach the point of spiritual maturity where we actually lost all desire to do evil? The ways of the worldly would simply be repulsive to us. A group of Church members over 2,000 years ago spoke of a "mighty change" within them that caused them to make a firm commitment to Christ that motivated them throughout the rest of their lives (see Mosiah 5:2). Nephi warns us that the outward ordinances of baptism and confirmation are not sufficient to ensure eternal life, but insists that we must "press forward with a steadfastness in Christ, . . . feasting upon the word of Christ, and endure to the end" (2 Nephi 31:19-21).

I think we as a people do not grasp the significance of the above-quoted passages. Only the Holy Ghost can enable us to understand just how fully we must repent and commit ourselves to the Lord. Those who are weak in faith and knowledge often rationalize to themselves just how much the Lord requires of us. Our desire is sufficient to begin the conversion process, but study and repentance and service are required to complete the journey. One cannot expect relief from the temptations of the flesh with half-hearted efforts at repentance or commitment. Carefully analyze this sobering statement by Joseph Fielding Smith:

> Baptism and confirmation into the Church do not necessarily insure our exaltation in the Kingdom of God. They do, provided we are true and faithful to every covenant and obligation required of us in the commandments of our Eternal Father. It is he who endures to the end who will be saved.
>
> However, it is my judgment that there are many members of this Church who have been baptized for the remission of their sins, and who have had hands laid upon their heads for the gift of the Holy Ghost, but who have never received that gift—that is, the manifestations of it. Why? Because they have never put themselves in order to receive these manifestations. They have never humbled themselves. They have never taken the steps that would prepare them for the companionship of the Holy Ghost. Therefore, they go through life without that knowledge; they are lacking in understanding. When those who are cunning and crafty in their deceit come to them criticizing the authorities of the Church and the doctrines of the Church, these weak members do not have understanding enough, information enough, and enough of the guidance of the Spirit of the Lord to resist false doctrines and teachings. They listen and think that perhaps they have made a mistake, and the first thing you know they find their way out of the Church, because they do not have understanding. (Joseph Fielding Smith, *Ensign,* June 1972, p. 3.)

I once received a long letter from a former member of the Church who had been converted to "Christianity." Her letter made it evident that she did not understand basic LDS doctrine. She had made the unfortunate decision to have her name removed from the records of the Church on the basis of that misunderstanding. I believe there are many in the Church, even among "active" members, who are easy prey for those who would deceive. Some turn away to other religious philosophies, such as the lady I have just described; others turn away from the standards of Christ completely to find a way of living that will allow for unrestricted sexual expression or other types of self-gratifying behaviors.

To fortify ourselves against such a possibility, we have the promise of the companionship of the Holy Ghost. That companionship can help us leap every hurdle and sidestep every roadblock in our quest for peace of mind. One of the most comforting passages of scripture for those who truly desire to do right was revealed to Joseph Smith in 1829. How do you suppose our friend Bob would feel if he were to ponder these words: "Therefore, fear not; . . . do good; let earth and hell combine against you, for if ye are built upon my rock, they cannot prevail. Behold, I do not condemn you; go your ways and sin no more. . . . Look unto me in every thought; doubt not, fear not. . . . Be faithful, keep my commandments, and ye shall inherit the kingdom of heaven." (D&C 6:34-37.)

The Power of the Ordinances

Doesn't it stand to reason that our Savior understands the difficulties of this life? I believe that he has the ability to comprehend and empathize with any and every predicament that a person living in the 1980s might encounter. Believing that, we ought to carefully consider what the Lord is telling us in the revelations. For example, he has taught us that the ordinances of the higher priesthood are given to help us come to know God (see D&C 84:19-22). The ordinances are divine channels through which man may receive knowledge and power to become like God.

The first ordinance is baptism, followed by the bestowal of the gift of the Holy Ghost. Later, after having proven themselves sufficiently, men can receive ordination to the Melchizedek Priesthood by an oath and a covenant (see D&C 84:35-40). The Melchizedek Priesthood is a prerequisite to enter the holy temple, where the higher ordinances of endowment and sealing prepare one even further to enter into exaltation. Young women receive the blessings of the priesthood in the house of the Lord when they are sealed to their husbands.

As a young missionary I was perplexed by a statement in my patriarchal blessing that indicated I had received the Melchizedek Priesthood, and that if I were true and faithful I would eventually receive the priesthood in its *fulness*. I thought being a worthy elder in the Melchizedek Priesthood was all I would need to get me and my family to the celestial kingdom. I discovered my misunderstanding the day my wife and I were sealed in the temple by Elder Franklin D. Richards. He explained that the fulness of the priesthood could only be enjoyed by a man and woman together. I could not have it without my wife Amaryllis, and she could not have it without me.

Through sacred ordinances we make solemn covenants to pattern our lives after the life of the Savior. But it is possible to forget the significance of these sacred ordinances and covenants as life goes on, so one of the primary tasks of mortality is to learn to remember—to remember who we are and what we have the potential to become. (Did you know that the word *remember* appears in some form or another 240 times in the Book of Mormon? President Spencer W. Kimball suggested that *remember* might be the most important word in the dictionary.)

One of the simplest and most familiar ordinances of the Church is the sacrament of the Lord's Supper. The Savior knew that it would be hard for us to remember the once-in-a-lifetime ordinance and covenant of baptism, so he provided the regular, weekly reminder, the sacrament, when we can build ourselves spiritually and regain an eternal perspective sometimes lost during a busy week. Unfortunately, many fail to take advantage of this sacred time of commitment when we can nourish our spirits.

After the Savior personally introduced the sacrament among the Nephites (see 3 Nephi 18:1-14), he taught them about prayer. Just as the sacrament can be a weekly and public time of commitment to Christ, prayer provides for a daily, even hourly, reminder of the promises we have made. The fact that prayer can be done in private increases the likelihood that we are sincere about our public commitments. Thus, covenants, ordinances, the sacrament, the temple, the priesthood, the Holy Ghost, and prayer help to keep us on the path that leads to happiness and joy in this life and to exaltation in eternity.

Moreover they increase our love for the Lord in this life. On that subject, Elder Howard W. Hunter said:

> He loves the Lord with all his heart who loves nothing in comparison of him, and nothing but in reference to him, who is ready to give up, do, or suffer anything in order to please and glorify him. He loves God with all his soul, or rather with all life, who is ready to give up life for his sake and to be deprived of the comforts of the world to glorify him. He loves God with all his strength who exerts all the powers of his body and soul in the service of God. He loves God with all his mind who applies himself only to know God and his will, who sees God in all things and acknowledges him in all ways. (*Improvement Era*, June 1965, p. 512.)

Control Your Environment

Our environment is whatever you and I choose to make it. It will include home, family circumstances, school, employment, play, sports, hobbies, books, magazines, music, television, movies, and plays—in other words, all the influences surrounding us.

One of the more familiar concerns regarding Church standards of dating, entertainment, and choice of friends is the notion that we need to mingle with the world in order to carry the gospel message to the rest of mankind. This is a fair assertion, for truly we must live *in* the world. The challenge remains, however, to avoid becoming *of* the world. Statistically, far too many of our youth find that the pull of the world is stronger than their own resolves.

I often ask young people, "How strong do you think you really are? Do you know your own areas of vulnerability? What precautions have you taken to ensure that you remain morally clean? How do you know that your friends who have lower standards will not succeed in lowering your standards?" Elder Neal A. Maxwell wrote, "Let us not company with fornicators—not because we are too good for them, but because . . . we are not good enough! Remember that bad situations can wear down even good people." (*Notwithstanding My Weakness* [Salt Lake City: Deseret Book Co., 1981], pp. 101-2.) When considering close relationships with those who abuse God's standards, remember this thought: "When playing near the mud with white gloves on, it's not usually the mud that gets glovey." We need to be wise in knowing when we can influence others for good, and when others are influencing us for ill.

Elder Maxwell points out that "Joseph had both good sense and good legs in fleeing from Potiphar's wife" (*Notwithstanding My Weakness*, p. 102). Generations rejoice in young Joseph's decision to flee from a tempting situation, although he had to suffer the immediate consequences, which, at the time, seemed so negative (see Genesis 39-41). Again, with historical hindsight, we groan inwardly as we read that King David allowed his passion the momentary gratification that resulted in such eternal regret (see 2 Samuel 11-12). Both Joseph and David found themselves in a tempting environment; but they made opposite decisions that typify the kinds of choices we face today.

Joseph was faithfully discharging his duty when temptation came to him, and he had the strength and good sense to flee. David, however, was alone in Jerusalem during the "time when kings go forth to battle" (2 Samuel 11:1). David sent Joab and all the other mighty men of Israel to defend their nation, but David tarried at Jerusalem; and when the temptation arose, he lacked the inner strength to resist.

Can you see the parallel regarding our environment today? There are times when we avoid our duty and place ourselves in tempting circumstances. For example, a group of young men may decide to skip the planned school or Church activity and end up watching a degrading movie at a drive-in theater. A young couple gives in to temptation at 2:00 A.M., when they should be asleep at their respective homes (or on their knees thanking God for an enjoyable evening). A traveling businessman finds himself at the hotel bar when he should have been in his room preparing for the next day's activities.

Do you remember my friend who changed employment rather than allow his working environment to slowly destroy his spirituality? That was not a sign of weakness—that was intelligence. There are few mortals on earth who can continue to resist any and all temptation if they constantly allow themselves to be bombarded with sexual stimuli.

In controlling your environment, be wise enough to accept the counsel of those who have a sincere regard for your welfare. Who cares most about your level of spirituality—your parents or the manager of the theater? Who is most concerned about your future marital happiness—your institute teacher or the author of the torrid romance novel? If one faces the prospect of the birth of a child out of wedlock, who shows the most understanding—your bishop, or the friend who suggests an abortion?

You must choose the course of your life. Choose wisely by being selective about the friends with whom you associate, the music you choose to listen to, the books or magazines you choose to read, the movies and television you watch, the places you go for entertainment, and the environment you choose to work in. I want to warn you in all sincerity to be selective about your environment. Every book, magazine, movie, song, dance, party, and friend must be worthy of you. You must be a wise judge!

Let's take music as an example. The evidence is overwhelming that much of today's music does not edify, and in many cases is destructive. Yet, many youth are convinced that such music does not have a negative effect on them. Lex de Azevedo responds to the young person who argues, "I've listened to these songs and it doesn't make me want to do anything wrong. It hasn't changed me, it hasn't affected me." He says:

> How do you know, how can you tell me that it hasn't affected you? You are standing here right now the result of all the thoughts

you've had, all the experiences, all the stimuli, that have come into your mind. How can you say this has not affected you?

You are what you are *because* of all of these things. Have you ever wondered, perhaps, why you may not be as spiritually motivated as you are, why your desire for righteousness isn't greater than it is? Is it because of the continuing bombardment from the telestial world that fills our minds with this telestial stimulus, that robs us of our Celestial desires? How can you say that it hasn't affected you?

Our brains are like computers. You put garbage in, you get garbage out. You put telestial input in and you get telestial behavior out. You put terrestrial input in and you get terrestrial behavior out. And if you put celestial input in, you will behave celestially and you will feel comfortable in inheriting a celestial world. Now many of us are into mixing it up. A little celestial input on Sunday, a few dirty movies during the week, a little telestial music, and do you know what, your brain works like a perfect micro processor. It sorts it all out and you come out somewhere in between. And that's probably why we are where we are right now. (Ricks College Devotional, 2 February 1982.)

Wise King Solomon repeatedly warned and taught the youth of his day to avoid certain situations. Read Proverbs 5:3-8; 6:23-28; and 7:1-27—which describe the prostitution and immorality facing the youth of Solomon's day—and determine for yourself how sound his counsel was, and is, even today. Unfortunately, Solomon did not follow his own counsel. He was persuaded by his wives to lower his standards in order to tolerate their religious desires. He built altars and places of worship for the heathen gods that some of his wives worshipped, and he gradually lost his own testimony. (See 1 Kings 11:1-6.)

On a positive note, it is interesting to realize that the ancient prophets, despite the wickedness they prophesied would occur in our day, also *yearned* for this time in which you and I live. Why? Certainly not for the evil that would prevail, but because of the widespread availability of truth and goodness to those who would seek it. No one needs to be engulfed in sin or worldliness unless they so choose—a choice that the youth who grew up in Sodom and Gomorrah did not have. Today, one can choose to be engulfed in the blessings of the restored gospel. That is what the ancient prophets envied about our time: the fulness of the gospel would be available to all nations, kindreds, tongues, and people. I cannot tell you all the good things you can do to have real joy, for there are so many wonderful things to do and think about in this life that I cannot number them.

You have such a good choice of worthwhile activities available to you if you will search them out and not be sidetracked by the cheap sideshows offered by those who do not understand the purpose of life. Seek after the good, the true, the virtuous, the praiseworthy—that which truly satisfies and leaves a good aftertaste. Then you will be prepared to fight and win the greatest battles, those which are fought in the mind.

9

It's the Thought That Counts

Most of us are very thankful for the relative privacy of our thoughts and desires. Can you imagine a video screen in your foreheads where every thought was broadcast for all to see in living color? Or how about a TV broadcasting unit over our hearts where every desire was open to all? One man said, "Make my heart transparent as pure crystal that the world, jealous of me, may see the foulest thought my heart does hold" (Byron Buckingham, quoted by Vaughn Featherstone, in *Purity of Heart* [Salt Lake City: Deseret Book Co., 1982], p. 98). Consider how others would feel toward us if they knew our thoughts and desires.

Every waking hour our mind is at work churning out thoughts and ideas, some resulting in words and actions. The Savior taught us to be clean by controlling our thoughts. He contrasted the higher law of the gospel with the lesser law of Moses by saying: "Ye have heard that it was said by them of old time, Thou shalt not commit adultery; but I say unto you, That whosoever looketh on a woman to lust after her hath committed adultery with her already in his heart" (Matthew 5:27-28). This passage has always caused young men to feel a bit uncomfortable. A latter-day Apostle has said that the greatest challenge to young people is to control their thoughts (see Elder Boyd K. Packer, *Ensign*, January 1974, p.

27). The Lord told Joseph Smith that those who lust in their thoughts "shall not have the Spirit, but shall deny the faith and shall fear" (D&C 63:16). I find three reasons for controlling my thoughts as I read that warning:

1. *Those with unclean thoughts shall not have the Spirit.* In the last chapter we read Joseph Fielding Smith's warning that there are many in the Church who have been baptized and confirmed, but who do not know what it is like to have the manifestation of the Holy Ghost. Those who continually allow their thought processes to dwell upon immoral fantasies and imaginings probably do not fully realize the price they are paying for such mental diversions: they disqualify themselves from the greatest gift to mortals.

2. *Those with unclean thoughts shall deny the faith.* Troy was a young man who wanted nothing to do with the Church. He was a deacon who had previously been involved in every aspect of Church commitment. His association with a new circle of friends in junior high school introduced him to pornography, and the talk that often goes on when young men fail to keep their lives involved in more worthwhile activities. Troy discontinued church attendance, personal and family prayer, and any other semblance of spiritual commitment, and competely disassociated himself from the gospel of Jesus Christ. In fact, he even refused to allow his family to refer to him as a member of the Church, and denied the existence of a God. Troy, in effect, denied his faith. Later, as he matured (and repented), he reestablished those ties with the Church and reopened the lines of communication with his Heavenly Father. Fortunately, he got his life back on course.

3. *Those with unclean thoughts shall fear.* I have wondered what exactly the Lord had in mind when he said we would *fear.* I thought of the fear-confidence feelings we have as we kneel in prayer. Could there be occasions when our lack of worthiness prevents us from calling on the Lord in a time of need? I shall never forget the feeling that swept over my entire being upon the realization that I had just backed our car over my five-year-old son Jared. As I jumped from the car and ran to the side of my son, I remember asking myself if I was worthy to give him a blessing to preserve

or even restore his life if necessary. He was not seriously hurt by the accident (we were in deep snow at the time), but I recall the hours and days of self-analysis that followed as I continued to ask myself, "What if . . .?"

Possibly the Lord's warning relates to interviews with our priesthood leaders. Fear would certainly be present in the heart of a person being interviewed for a temple recommend or a Church calling, whose thoughts were often dominated by lust. And, of course, the bishop's interview is only a prelude to that final interview when we account for our words and deeds and thoughts to God himself. I can't think of anything that would enable us to enjoy life and be prepared for whatever surprises life may bring our way than to have confidence, rather than fear, toward the future. Clean thoughts are the source of such a positive outlook on life.

Thought Precedes Action

Most people today would argue, "I have a hard enough time just controlling my actions without trying to keep my thoughts in line too." What they fail to understand is the relationship between thoughts and actions. "As he thinketh in his heart, so is he" (Proverbs 23:7). People would have less of a struggle controlling their actions if they refused to contemplate evil in their minds.

Truman Madsen wrote an interesting parable that illustrates the need to decisively win the battles in our minds:

Herman Vermin

There once lived a rat named Herman Vermin down by the Old Mill Tread.

He was a rat in the usual maze. But that was not the problem. It was the maze in the rat.

What bothered him was his thoughts. He watched organized crime on TV and wondered how it would be to catch his enemies in *his* trap. He saw sensational wickedness on billboards and at the movies and found it fascinating. He read a lot of rot about dirty rats, imagining what it would be like to be like them. And then there were his thoughts about flopsy and curvy girl rats. "How would you like to be pasted in my scrapbook," he would say under his breath.

97

Now Herman may have looked white through all this, but down deep he was embarrassed, a real reddened rodent. In the throes of it, he often felt dull and dense and couldn't concentrate. He had the gnawing feeling that he should talk his problem out with someone wise. But whom could he trust? He would only shake up his friends. So, he figured, if he didn't indulge these fantasies all the time—at least not while in Church—and if he was careful to keep his trap shut, no one could say he was any worse than his brother rats.

Then came a revelation.

A great white one who had emerged from the Tread Mill discerned his anxiety. He was full of a contagious peace of mind and soul.

He told Herman that the greatest thing he could ever learn was this: Not the occurrence of thoughts in one's head but their lodgment in his heart corrupts. The issue is not whether we contemplate evil, but whether we crave it. The ideal is to see through evil, and beyond it, and to overcome its pulling power in our nature.

Most of us, he went on, control our thoughts by trying to replace them with good thoughts. That is wise.

But there is a more penetrating way. And that is to bring our whole inner warfare out into the light, the light of prayer! In no other way can the poison of evil desires be purged, and thoughts be released toward what is creative and not destructive.

For the first time, Herman began to understand the meaning of the ancient saying, "Unto the pure all things are pure."

MORAL: "Look unto Me in every thought. Doubt not. Fear not." (D&C 6:36)

Even the great Old Testament prophet Job, a man the Lord described as a perfect and upright man (see Job 1:1), apparently had to face the need to control his thoughts, for he speaks of having "made a covenant" with his eyes, and asks, "Why then should I think upon a maid?" (Job 31:1). If you struggle with controlling your thoughts, you are not alone. Remember, "Not the occurrence of thoughts in one's head but their lodgment in his heart corrupts." I recall President Marion G. Romney saying, "You may not be able to keep a bird from landing on your head, but you can sure keep it from building a nest there."

I once attended a Young Adult conference in Cookeville, Tennessee. Our special guest was President Spencer W. Kimball. One thing stands out in my memory regarding that visit. He asked us to sing a hymn with him. He said it was one of his favorites. President Kimball then quoted the words to that hymn before we sang it. I shall never forget the feeling and intensity in his voice as he said, "I need thee, O, I need thee, every hour I need thee!" It was like a revelation to me. "That's it," I thought. "President Kimball's success in life stems from his complete and total reliance on the Lord!" He was teaching us that we could not afford to take even a one-hour vacation from the Lord's Spirit. Every *hour* I need thee! I thought of how many times we allow a Saturday evening movie or television program to dampen the spirit of the Sabbath day. How many hours spent reading "innocent" novels or magazines have subtly retarded our spiritual growth?

The Lord was speaking in earnest when he said, "Look unto me in *every* thought" (D&C 6:36; emphasis added). We allow many destructive influences to invade the privacy of our minds. I like Elder Boyd K. Packer's analogy of the mind being compared to a vacant lot:

> I have the idea that many go through life with their minds something like a corner lot at a city intersection, just a lot on which there is no house. It's used for many things — children cross it to play, people cross it going here and there, sometimes a car will take a shortcut across it. Here is a mind, a vacant playing field; and anyone who comes by can crisscross it. I don't have that anymore. On my lot I have some signs that say No Trespassing, and then I list to whom that refers. I will not consent to contamination of the slightest single spot from a perverse source. I will not consent to it. If a thought like that enters my mind, it comes as a trespasser; it comes as an unwanted intruder. I do consent openly — without reservation, hopefully, with anxiety, pleadingly, with all invitation — to inspiration from the Lord.
>
> Now I just ask you, do you have your No Trespassing signs up? Do you have your relationship with yourself and your relationship with the Lord established to the point that you have declared to whom you will listen and to whom you will not? Well, lots of influences come to the edge of the property, and they try to find a path

that isn't marked. Once in a while they find a new one, and then I am busy making another sign to guard that one too, because I have my agency and I will not consent. I will not.

I will not consent to any influence from the adversary. I have come to know what power he has. I know all about that. But I also have come to know the power of truth and of righteousness and of good, and I want to be good. I'm not ashamed to say that—I want to be good. And I've found in my life that it has been critically important that this was established between me and the Lord so that I knew that he knew which way I committed my agency. I went before him and said, "I'm not neutral, and you can do with me what you want. If you need my vote, it's there. I don't care what you do with me, and you don't have to take anything from me because I give it to you—everything, all I own, all I am—"and that makes the difference. ("To Those Who Teach In Troubled Times," in *The Charge to Religious Educators,* Religion 370 Institute Manual [Church Educational System], p. 71.)

Christ, of course, is a "discerner of the thoughts and intents of the heart" (D&C 33:1), and when we come to understand and believe that he was "in all points tempted like as we are" (Hebrews 4:15), then we begin to glimpse the fact that he is the solution to the struggle. He literally understands every challenge with evil for he "descended below all things . . . that he might be in all and through all things, the light of truth" (D&C 88:6). Only by laying all on the altar before Christ can we fully appreciate the purifying influence he can have on our life.

The Conscience and the Ability to Remember

How can we have the purifying influence of the Lord in our life? First, recognize the close relationship between our conscience and the promptings of the Spirit. President Kimball has written, "Conscience tells the individual when he is entering forbidden worlds, and it continues to prick until silenced by the will or by sin's repetition" (*New Era,* Nov. 1980, p. 41). The conscience seems to be a repository for all the good, the pure, the ethical, the proper, and the truthful things we have learned from all sources during our lifetime. It is generally assumed that the conscience is the Light of Christ which is given to *every* man (see Moroni 7:16; D&C 84:46). The Holy Ghost is a greater light given in addition to the conscience as a permanent gift when one is confirmed a member of the Church of Jesus Christ. I believe that when we heed our conscience, we are also heeding the Holy Ghost.

Second, we can do those things that will enable us to *remember.* Elder Neal A. Maxwell said, "I believe that sin is a special form of insanity, that it reflects a kind of 'blackout' in which we either lack perspective about the consequence of our thoughts, words, and actions, or we lose it temporarily" (*Ensign,* Apr. 1974, p. 21). It would seem helpful, then, to fill our days with those kinds of activities that would help us to keep our perspective. Do you remember Tevye, in *Fiddler on the Roof,* explaining why the Jewish people had so many traditions? *They help them remember who they are and what God expects of them.* Latter-day Saints, like the Jews, have many traditions—family home evenings, personal and family prayers, scripture study, welfare service, home teaching, seminary, family reunions, etc.—which enable us to remember who we are and what God expects of us.

Peter taught the Saints of the early-day Church the principles that enable us to become godlike and make our calling and election sure. He warns, "He that lacketh those things is blind, and cannot see afar off, and hath forgotten that he was purged from his old sins" (2 Peter 1:9). Doesn't that accurately describe the state of those who lose sight of who they really are? Peter then continues to teach that he will strive continually to keep the Saints in remembrance of these things. In fact, he promises that he will even make arrangements for them to be reminded of these truths after his death. That promise was realized as millions have read his words of reminder in the Bible.

Nephi is especially sensitive as to how we can remember to stay on the strait and narrow way: "And now . . . I suppose that ye ponder somewhat in your hearts concerning that which ye should do after ye have entered in by the way" (2 Nephi 32:1). Nephi recommends three sources of strength:

1. *Ponder the scriptures.* "Feast upon the words of Christ; for behold, the words of Christ will tell you all things what ye should do" (2 Nephi 32:3).

2. *Receive the Holy Ghost.* "If ye will enter in by the way, and receive the Holy Ghost, it will show unto you all things what ye should do" (2 Nephi 32:5).

3. *Pray always.* "I say unto you that ye must pray always; . . . that thy performance may be for the welfare of thy soul" (2 Nephi 32:9).

Nephi's brother Jacob uses an interesting phrase, *firmness of mind,* in his great sermon to the Saints of his day. Notice the qualities necessary to qualify oneself as pure in heart: "I, Jacob, would speak unto you that are pure in heart. Look unto God with *firmness of mind,* and pray unto him with exceeding faith, and he will console you in your afflictions, and he will plead your cause. . . . O all ye that are pure in heart, lift up your heads and receive the pleasing word of God, and feast upon his love; for ye may, if your *minds are firm,* forever." (Jacob 3:1-2; emphasis added.)

Thus we find the prophets in agreement concerning those things that will enable us to cultivate a close relationship with the Godhead. Prayer, pondering the scriptures, sensitivity to the Spirit, and similar daily habits, open the door to divine influence and block out the negative influences of the adversary.

I must add one caution, and that is the possibility of doing all the "right" things (reading the scriptures, attending church, praying, etc.), and still not receiving the promised strength. All of these things must be preceded by strong desire, proper motives, sincerity of heart, and the commitment to Christ of which we spoke in the preceding chapter. Impatience in receiving the promised blessings causes many to falter and conclude that their efforts were in vain. Look up *patience* and *endure* in the Topical Guide of the LDS edition of the Bible, and notice how critical these qualities are for those who desire the blessings of the Lord. Time is one of those factors that the Lord uses to refine and strengthen our depth of commitment to him. To the degree we control our thoughts and desires, we will find the temptation toward immorality lessened.

You might find the following list of suggestions on ways to control your thoughts (submitted by students in an institute class on the Life of Christ) helpful to you:

1. Think of hymns or scriptural passages.

2. Learn to let negative thoughts enter one ear and fly out the other. "You may not be able to keep a bird from landing on your head, but you can sure keep it from building a nest there." Don't dwell on the negative.

3. Serve: do something for someone else.

4. Fill your mind with positive, uplifting, and inspiring thoughts and stories by reading good books, the *Ensign, New Era,* and others.

5. Exercise: do something physically demanding.

6. Exercise self-discipline in various areas of your life: arise early, study regularly, eat properly, etc.

7. Fast and pray.

8. Get a special priesthood blessing from your father, husband, or priesthood leader.

9. Be organized and prepared in your life, and avoid frustrations.

10. Avoid indecision: do what you must when you know you should.

11. Fill your private moments with positive thoughts. What do you think about when you don't have to think about anything?

12. To the degree that you can, structure your environment to screen out those influences and stimulations that are negative.

13. Have clearly defined goals and purposes each day.

14. Remind yourself of the rewards for thinking positive thoughts: a mission, marriage, children, your reputation, seeing the Savior face to face (see D&C 88:67-68).

15. Read the scriptures daily.

10

Thou Shalt Not Fly Thy Airplane into the Trees

The title of this chapter comes from an outstanding address by Elder Hartman Rector, Jr., in the October 1972 general conference. You might want to read the entire talk, but let me share just a brief excerpt:

> In my experience, I have found that it is very, very dangerous to fly just high enough to miss the treetops. I spent twenty-six years flying the Navy's airplanes. It was very exciting to see how close I could fly to the trees. This is called "flat-hatting" in the Navy, and it is extremely dangerous. When you are flying just high enough to miss the trees and your engine coughs just once, you are in the trees.
>
> Now let's pretend that the Navy had a commandment—"Thou shalt not fly thy airplane in the trees." As a matter of fact, they did have such a commandment. In order to really be free of the commandment, it becomes necessary for me to add a commandment of my own to the Navy's commandment, such as, "Thou shalt not fly thy airplane closer than 5,000 feet to the trees." When you do this, you make the Navy's commandment of not flying in the trees easy to live, and the safety factor is tremendously increased. (*Ensign,* Jan. 1973, p. 131.)

The commandment to be morally clean is as important to our eternal welfare as keeping the airplane out of the trees would be to a pilot's physical welfare. I am sure you can see the obvious parallel. We must each make our own list of commandments designed to help us keep the Lord's overall commandment. Our list of personal commandments should prevent us from being overcome by temptation in a moment of weakness or forgetfulness.

For example, Jennie's personal commandment might be, "I'll never go on another date with Alvin." One would search in vain to find that commandment in the scriptures; yet based on her past experience with Alvin, she knows that to be alone with him would be foolish. The Holy Ghost (or her conscience) warns her in advance, based upon her own particular weaknesses. Carl wrote the following in his list of commandments: "I will not watch . . ." (a television show that lowers his spirituality whenever he views it). As you think about your own strengths, weaknesses, and circumstances, you should be able to write your own list of commandments that will enable you to keep the Lord's commandment to be chaste. (See chapter 11, exercise 12, for ways to make the commandments fit your situation.)

If you are serious about living a life of purity, you will fortify yourself now against the challenges that will come. There are many wise Church leaders, counselors, teachers, and social scientists who have developed various strategies for controlling the physical expression of affection before marriage, and keeping such expression within the bounds the Lord has set after marriage. The remainder of this chapter contains a summary of three helpful approaches.

How's Your Appetite?

A popular approach among many LDS teachers is Kenneth Hardy's "appetitional" explanation of sexual motivation (see *Psychological Review,* 71:1, 1964, pp. 1-18; also condensed in Kenneth Cannon's *Developing A Marriage Relationship,* BYU, 1972, pp. 179-92). Dr. Hardy's theory makes a lot of sense to those who recognize free agency as the ruling principle of our existence (see D&C 93:30). The sexual drive is based not only upon biological instinct, but primarily on *learned* behavior. As we experience various sexual stimuli, we develop an appetite for those things that are rewarding or pleasurable. Furthermore, as we repeat a pleasurable activity, we require increased stimulation in order to receive the same degree of pleasure that we experienced initially.

For example, Dr. Hardy's theory would predict that it will be much more exciting for Alvin to hold Jennie's hand on their first date than it will on their fifth date. I recall the anticipation and reward of holding my wife's hand for the first time. We attended a football game on our first date and I grabbed her hand to keep us from being separated as we squeezed through the ticket gate with the crowd. Her response was most gratifying (she did not let go for the next two hours). As we continued to date, I still enjoyed holding hands, but we naturally desired other forms of intimacy— an arm around the waist, a hug, a kiss. We both recognized that certain expressions of intimacy were reserved for marriage, and wisely set limits on the kinds of affection we would allow ourselves to experience.

Unfortunately, many fail to recognize that exposure to sexually provocative activities or stimuli will only make it more difficult to control their actions in the future. According to Dr. Hardy, appetites are developed in youth through the following practices: (1) early dating; (2) steady dating early in the courtship years; (3) dating practices characterized by chronic love-making; (4) exposure to sexually stimulating materials such as suggestive or obscene literature and movies, etc.; (5) the lowering of those moral standards that promote self-discipline.

The obvious implication of Dr. Hardy's analysis is that we should wisely determine our values, and then restrict those activities which would make it more difficult to maintain those values. Many young people today attend sexually explicit movies, engage in necking or petting, or read inappropriate magazines or books, and then wonder why the sexual drives within them seem almost impossible to control! The mental and spiritual conflict associated with physical gratifications that violate our moral standards—such as guilt arising from masturbation, impure thoughts, or necking

107

and petting—can be eliminated by removing the sources of stimulation and altering our behavior to fit our standards. Unfortunately, today's permissive society makes it much easier to remove the guilt by merely lowering the standards.

There is a tremendous value in naiveté (lacking worldliness or sophistication). The word *naive* is often used as a term of derision directed toward one who is unaware of the ways of the world. By avoiding experiences that may make us "worldly wise," we do ourselves a great service.

Consider two LDS missionaries entering the home of an investigator to present a gospel discussion. Elder Macho had "been around," but eventually desired to serve a mission and obtain the spiritual blessings of eternity. Elder Naive, on the other hand, was so innocent that his friends used to call him "lily-white" and "the bishop" before his mission. Both now desire to live in tune with the Holy Ghost. Both are seeking to purify and sanctify their minds and hearts.

As they enter the home to present a lesson, they find the woman they are to teach very attractive and immodestly dressed. According to Dr. Hardy's theory, Elder Macho would not only have to deal with the immediate stimuli before him, but might also find old experiences and desires of the past aroused at a most inconvenient time.

It is true that forgiveness for past transgression is complete when preceded by complete repentance, but that does not always guarantee a removal of past memories that must be continually kept under control (at least in this life). It could be likened unto the reformed alcoholic who continues to find the smell of alcohol desirable, or the former coffee drinker who still craves a cup of aromatic coffee on a cold morning.

Dr. Hardy's appetitional theory suggests the following recommendations for controlling lust during the premarital period:

  1. Participation in activities which fill one's life with abundant gratifications, so that sexual intimacies are not indulged in as an escape from boredom or emotional starvation. (See chapter 11, exercise 10.)

2. Comprehension to the nature of sex motivation and the factors which govern it, to help the person to foresee the consequences of alternative courses of action, thus enabling him to make a knowledgeable decision in terms of his own motives and values. (That's what this chapter is designed to help you do.)

3. Abstinence from arousing activities until the time acceptable for sexual expression, to prevent the appetite from growing. This implies a dating-courtship pattern (group dating, creative dating) which is centered upon a wide variety of nonsexual activities which additionally might contribute to a more adequate prediction of marital compatability.

4. Exposure to entertainment, reading material, and companionship which have nonsexual connotations, and are of interest to you. (See chapter 11, exercises 3, 4, and 6.)

5. Emphasis upon the long-term rewards of continence (self-control), and idealization of the ability to delay immediate gratification of impulse. (See chapter 11, exercises 3, 7, 8, and 9.)

Dr. Hardy's theory also provides insight for sexual compatibility in marriage. There are those who argue that couples need to experiment sexually before marriage to determine their degree of compatibility, since it is of such importance to successful marriage adjustment. Dr. Hardy maintains that a couple achieves sexual compatibility through mutual adjustment until appetites and desires are harmonious and appropriate. One's appetite is not biologically static; rather it is controlled by our attitudes and experiences. Sexual adjustment in marriage is a natural consequence of a couple's nonsexual love for each other.

Commitment to Each Other — A Communication Approach

After a five-month engagement, Sandy and Mike were ready to get married. Due to a medical problem that required immediate surgery for Mike, the wedding was postponed for three months.

During the recuperation period (which set an indoor record for that type of surgery), Mike couldn't work or go to school, so the days and evenings were spent with his sweetheart, planning their life together. Their physical attraction for each other was strong, and it became more difficult to say goodnight as the summer dragged on. Both recognized the need to maintain the highest standards of courtship, for they had both been to the temple previously and wanted to return in worthiness for their marriage.

While sitting on a blanket behind Sandy's apartment one Sunday afternoon, they talked about the remaining six weeks before they would marry and the increasing physical pressures they had both felt.

"I have a suggestion," Sandy said, with a twinkle in her eye. "Since we both recognize the need to avoid getting too physically involved, why don't we make an agreement to just hold hands — and no more — until we are married?"

Mike's laugh in reply was partly a response to a good joke, and partly a fear that she was really serious. "You know you couldn't resist me for that long," he quipped.

"But Mike," she countered, "We know how we feel about each other. We don't have to prove anything. I think we can do it!"

Mike chewed on a piece of grass for a few minutes while he absorbed the implications of her suggestion. Finally he replied, "I suppose it would make waiting for August 18 a lot easier. And, besides, it really would be interesting to see if we could exercise that kind of self-control. We could do it if we were separated by a thousand miles. Let's prove to ourselves just how strong our commitment to each other can be!"

After a brief discussion, they finally agreed on Mike's suggestion that in addition to holding hands, a single goodnight kiss (very brief) would be the only other expression of physical affection allowable. As Mike drove to his apartment that evening, he felt a closeness to Sandy and to God that was new and stronger than anything he had previously experienced. The remaining weeks were the most enjoyable of their courtship, without the temptation and pressures they had been experiencing prior to their commitment. On August 18, they knelt across the altar in the Salt Lake Temple, dressed in white, as the Lord's servant joined them for time and eternity. Their marriage was sealed by the Holy Spirit of Promise, for they were *worthy!* (Elder O. Leslie Stone defines what it means to be sealed by the Holy Spirit of Promise in *New Era,* Nov. 1971, p. 6.)

Today their marriage is characterized by trust and faith in each other, even during times of stress and trial, for they laid the proper foundation of commitment to each other and to God in their courtship. Sandy and Mike weren't aware of it at the time, but they were following some basic principles of communication that have been taught by Dr. Lynn Scoresby, a marriage and family therapist and instructor at BYU. Regarding the challenge of setting limits on premarital sexual expression, Dr. Scoresby teaches serious couples to follow three simple steps:

1. *Establish mutuality.* Mutuality means that both the male and female take equal responsibility in setting limits. Within this context Dr. Scoresby shares an interesting definition of leadership. Leadership is "doing the right thing that needs to be done before someone else has to do it." It is the leader who says, "let's stop" or "let's talk." In the case of Sandy and Mike, leadership was demonstrated when Sandy said, "I have a suggestion."

2. *Define what is meant by various kinds of nonverbal behavior.* What did Mike mean when he kissed Sandy goodnight? Most couples have never thought about the possible meaning of such intimacies. For example, a goodnight kiss *could* mean "I like you very much. In fact, I have never felt so attracted to another person before." Or, a goodnight kiss might mean "I guess I owe him a kiss since he spent $20 of his hard-earned money on me." Or, a goodnight kiss might be merely the expected prelude to what one might hope will occur later, such as heavy necking or petting.

Does a desire for physical closeness represent feelings of love? Or do such desires stem from purely physical desires of lust? It may be uncomfortable to discuss such questions, but remember we are suggesting this communication approach for those couples who have reached a high level of commitment, such as steady dating preceding possible engagement, or during the period of engagement itself. Couples who cannot communicate about feelings and motives *before* marriage are not likely to have much success *after* marriage.

3. *Set explicit limits.* When both partners have shared their feelings and motives regarding physical intimacy, it is necessary to reach agreement on clearly defined limits, beyond which neither will venture. Included in this third step is what action is to be taken if either or both exceed the limits. For example, if a couple has been involved in heavy necking or petting and then commits to set their limit to one goodnight kiss, they may decide in advance to spend two weeks without any contact if one or the other tries to go beyond the limits. Such a consequence would enable them to think about the importance of commitments and possibly enable a couple to break destructive patterns of behavior that could interfere with their preparation for marriage. In extreme cases, a couple might agree to terminate the relationship if self-control cannot be maintained.

This strategy can have two possible results. If both partners are able to wisely discuss intimacy, set limits, and live up to those limits, they are proving to each other the depth of their love for each other and the Lord. They are also laying a foundation of trust and integrity for their future marriage.

On the other hand, let us suppose that a young man consistently makes promises verbally, and then breaks them during moments of temptation and desire. The girl may rightly conclude that her prospective husband may lack the self-discipline necessary to lead their family. She may come to realize that his own selfish desires are more important to him than a promise to maintain their agreed-on standard. A young man may possibly detect a lack of spiritual sensitivity on the part of that beautiful young lady he thought he might like to marry. In these circumstances, a couple would be wise to think carefully and go slowly before allowing a wedding ceremony to carry such weaknesses into the marriage.

You may find it difficult to begin such communication with your steady dating partner or fiancé, but once the ice has been broken, it will be easier. One might say, during an especially good time together: "I want to talk to you about something that is very important to both of us, something that's not easy for me to discuss. Is this a good time for you?" Proceed to define your own nonverbal behavior, your feelings and expressions of affection, and what they mean to you. Then ask your partner how he or she feels. After you have both had opportunity to discuss the relationship, it is necessary for one to propose some explicit limits. Through discussion, both can come to an agreement. All that remains is to determine what action will be taken if those limits are not observed. It might also be agreed that a certain procedure could be followed for modifying the limits if circumstances change (but certainly not in the middle of a romantic evening together!).

Developing the above-described skills will be helpful in your future marriage and also in any situation that requires communication, commitment, and genuine regard for another person or group.

Hope for the Hopeless

Most leaders who teach or counsel have become acquainted with young people or older adults who have serious problems with sexual deviancy. Often there are emotional and spiritual factors related to problems such as homosexuality, compulsive masturbation, or promiscuity, which have been years in developing before the person ever begins to seek help. In my own experience, I have found many who felt powerless to change their behavior—especially after they have tried and failed repeatedly. I have several suggestions for such individuals.

First, make a close friend of your bishop. (See chapter 4 for an explanation of the role of a bishop in the repentance process.) The ultimate solution to the problems of life are spiritual, and your bishop not only holds the keys of a Judge in Israel, but he can direct you to many sources of help—the Holy Ghost, the scriptures, and professional therapy, if needed. Unfortunately, many who are having prolonged and serious problems of unchastity have ceased to associate themselves closely with the Church. They feel too uncomfortable, yet they cannot live peaceably with themselves, knowing what they are doing about their potential and purpose in life.

My second suggestion, then, is to seek assistance from a competent counselor who understands and accepts the LDS perspective on the nature of man, human free agency, and our ultimate destiny. Such an individual can provide not only the psychological expertise, but will often help to restore one's confidence and feelings of self worth to the point that the transgressor will again turn to the true source of all strength, which is eternal.

Dr. Allen Bergin, BYU professor of psychology, wrote an article entitled "Toward a Theory of Human Agency," which was condensed and printed in the *New Era* (July 1973, pp. 33-41). I rejoiced as I recognized in Dr. Bergin one who not only had the intellectual credentials to provide help for those who seem to have lost all semblance of self-control, but also demonstrated an understanding and commitment to spiritual truths that must be included in any attempt to help people in an eternal way. Dr. Bergin wrote:

> There is nothing more pitiful than the person who wants to control his behavior but is unable to do so. Such individuals are buffeted by their own fears and impulses; their behavior is dominated by Satan. In such instances, self-effort alone will not suffice.

When people have repeatedly resisted the Light of Christ, their conscience, or the Holy Ghost, they have allowed Satan to have an increased influence in their life and they lose a portion of their agency. Dr. Bergin's studies with several cases involving compulsive homosexuality yielded some helpful insights. In these extreme cases, it is necessary to have the assistance of others "who temporarily aid the person in establishing new levels of control that could not be achieved by self-effort alone. . . . Simply telling a person to 'go control himself' will not do."

It was observed that loss of self-control (in other words transgression) occurred because the attempt to control behavior was applied late in the sequence of events when emotional and physical arousal was high. The clients were taught to identify tempting

114

stimuli such as thought patterns, environmental situations, and so on, much earlier, and consciously choose to go in a different direction.

Most of us do not take early warning signals very seriously. A thought, a glance, a touch, or a picture may not be dangerous alone, but coupled with additional stimuli, they start us on a slow descent in spirituality which may result in transgression down the road. How much easier for an alcoholic to resist the *thought* of a drink, than to resist drinking a glass of alcohol sitting on the table in front of him. Consider Cheryl LeBaron's descriptive analogy: "It's like the fat guy who goes to the refrigerator, opens it, takes out some thick bread, butter, salami, cheese, lettuce, tomatoes, and pickles, a quart of milk, and half of a chocolate cake, arranges them on the table, sits down, says the blessing, and *then* decides whether or not he ought to eat" (*Chastity, Now and Forever* [Salt Lake City: RIC Publishing Co., 1981], pp. 17-18).

By identifying turning points earlier, we have sufficient will power to make correct choices before emotional or physical desires dominate. President David O. McKay often said, "The greatest battles of our life are fought within the silent chambers of our own souls." In the case of serious problems, a professional therapist can slowly and carefully teach his clients how to use their own free agency. I am grateful for therapists, bishops, teachers, and parents who take the time and energy necessary to help those who seemingly have lost (temporarily) the ability to help themselves.

Often a person is so ashamed of his or her weakness that they cut themselves off from the very sources of strength they need most. A parent is often the last person a struggling youth will turn to. But in most cases, parents would be the single most helpful source of assistance. The nature of some weaknesses require not just one instance of confession and commitment, but rather repeated follow-up that will gradually enable the transgressor to build spirituality and resist temptation. A parent is in the best position to provide regular, even daily or hourly support.

I have had students come to me privately following a class discussion which gave them hope. Where serious sin has occurred, I have encouraged them to make contact with their bishop. In some

115

instances, they have been to several bishops and others over the years, and yet still struggle with their problem. At such times, I lament my own lack of ability, my limited understanding of the human mind and body, and recognize that some people need professional counseling that I am not qualified to give.

I love to see the light of hope in the eyes of those who sense anew their own ability to be masters of their destiny. A student wrote, after conquering a major weakness in his life: "My problems became serious when I swallowed Satan's lie—that once I had transgressed, it wouldn't hurt to do it once more. Nothing could have been further from the truth. Today, I know that I must not rationalize and make exceptions. And when I make mistakes, I repent quickly!"

There is no weakness in having problems. We all have problems. Weakness comes in refusing to admit we are weak, or refusing to do anything about our weaknesses. When we feel too weak or discouraged to do what needs to be done on our own, we must have the wisdom to turn to a trusted friend, parent, priesthood leader, or professional counselor who will help us help ourselves.

11

Write Your Own Chapter

Only you can write the conclusion to this book. If you have read this far, you have surely had some ideas and impressions relating to your own life. I hope you will take some time to write the thoughts and feelings you have on this important subject of purity.

Before you do that, however, I want to give you a few thoughts on the Holy Ghost. My experience with youth and young adults (and most adults, for that matter) has revealed that most members of the Church do not have confidence in their own ability to receive revelation for their lives. It is easy to accept the experiences of others—parents, teachers, leaders, or General Authorities—but we falter in believing and recognizing revelation from God meant just for us! Possibly it is because we misunderstand the nature of revelation. The Lord revealed to Joseph Smith and Oliver Cowdery that he would speak to us by the Holy Ghost in our *minds* and in our *hearts* (see D&C 8:2), and that this qualified as revelation in the same sense as Moses directing the Children of Israel.

The "voice" of God spoke the following words to a young man: "Enos, thy sins are forgiven thee, and thou shalt be blessed" (Enos 1:5). Later, in that same small book, we learn that the "voice" came to Enos, not through his ears, but to his *mind* (see Enos 1:10). I am suggesting that the Lord speaks to us more often

117

than we realize, through mental ideas and feelings of the heart—often through our conscience. At times, the message will be so clear that we can actually quote the Lord! I recall one occasion when I was pondering and praying over a matter involving one of my children. At one point in my prayer, several ideas flooded into my consciousness. I knew I had just been given the inspiration I desired, so I quickly thanked the Lord, ended my prayer, and went immediately to my desk and recorded those impressions into my journal so that I would not forget them.

As you write in your journal, learn to listen carefully to your mind, your heart, and your conscience. Write down what you hear and feel. You will find an increased ability to distinguish between your own desires and those that come from the Lord—between your own ideas, and those prompted by the Spirit. As you write by inspiration, you will be able to have confidence in the course of life you take. I am positive that you will feel a great outpouring of the Spirit at times which will bring with it a strengthening of your resolves to be pure.

President Spencer W. Kimball has written, "If we would avoid the danger spots which lead to transgression and sorrow and to forfeiture of our chances for exaltation, the wise way is to chart the course of our lives" (*The Miracle of Forgiveness*, p. 233). It is now time to chart your course. You will need a notebook, your journal, or just some blank sheets of paper. Look at the following exercises. Read the thought questions, ponder them in light of your particular circumstances, and then answer them in writing. If you are as busy as most people are today, you will be tempted to just close the book and slowly forget it. Please resist that temptation, or this book will be of no more value to you than a mediocre Sunday evening fireside. You will find that reading, thinking, and then writing your thoughts will have a much greater impression on your attitudes and behavior than mere reading alone would have.

Exercise 1
Where Am I Now?

Write a sentence, a paragraph, or a page in answer to the following three questions regarding the law of chastity:

1. What is your *understanding* of the Lord's law of chastity? What do you think the Lord means when he expects a chaste people?
2. What are your *feelings* regarding the law of chastity? Positive? Negative? Mixed? Confused?
3. How well do you measure up in *behavior* regarding the law of chastity (thoughts and actions)? This is a very personal question, and you may want to think it through and write it in your mind rather than on paper.

Exercise 2
Who Cares?

Make a list of 20 or more people who want you to be morally clean. (Some have a list of over 100!) When you finish, make another list of people who "couldn't care less." Compare the two lists.

Who Cares?	Who "Couldn't Care Less"?

Exercise 3
Looking Ahead!

Make a list of possible goals or experiences you could have in the future — such as temple marriage — that would require that you be morally clean. Put a star or asterisk beside those that are especially important to you.

Exercise 4
Whom Can I Trust?

Make a list of various sources that you would rely on for guidance on the subject of chastity, dating, marriage, and parenthood. Think of specific people — friends, relatives, teachers, leaders, and others; also think of educational sources such as specific books, magazines, texts, and TV programs. Then make another list of sources you would feel cautious or uneasy about accepting advice from on these same subjects.

Sources I Can Trust	Sources I Would Be Cautious About

Exercise 5
Some Hard Questions to Answer

Suppose you are faced with a present or future decision to engage in some type of unchaste behavior. How would you answer each of the following questions?

1. Do you know as much about sex and your own emotions as you think you do?
2. If you were to break the moral code, how would you feel tomorrow? In 10 years? In 500 years?
3. Are you considering this action because you are afraid of losing her (him)? If she (he) rejects you for your high standards, what have you really lost?
4. Are you trying to prove your independence from your parents? Another person? The Church? Who will suffer the most for your independence?
5. You have just completed giving a lecture to a college class on proper preparation for the future. The following question is posed by a student. "We are constantly hearing all of the fear statistics regarding premarital sex (venereal disease, pregnancy, abortion, etc.). Are there some *positive* reasons for chastity?" Summarize in writing your answer.

Exercise 6
Controlling My Environment

Make a list of at least twenty activities or experiences that will build you spiritually and strengthen your resolve to be morally clean. Include five worthwhile books or magazines and five uplifting television shows or movies.

Then make a list of at least twenty activities or experiences you must avoid if you hope to grow spiritually. Include five books or magazines and five television shows that you personally know you must avoid.

Exercise 7
Someday I Will Marry . . .

Make a list of ten or more specific qualities you want in your future husband or wife. Even though you may not have met him (her) yet, would you care what he (she) did this coming Friday night on a date? Would you care whether or not he (she) was involved in necking or petting? Do you suppose your future spouse (wherever he or she may be today) cares about your thoughts and actions at this time of your life?

After completing the list, go through it again and rate yourself on how well you are doing on each one of those qualities.

Exercise 8
. . . And Be A Parent!

Do you feel an obligation to your children yet unborn? What heritage of purity do you hope to pass on to your future children—and hence to generations beyond? What will you name your future sons and daughters? If your teen should one day ask you, "Dad (Mom), were you morally clean when you were my age?" How would you like to respond?

Write a paragraph outlining your advice to your teenage son or daughter on the subject of courtship and dating.

Exercise 9
The Iron Rod!

Review your scripture index or Topical Guide under the headings of "Purity," "Chastity," and "Virtue," and review scriptural passages or stories that seem to be particularly meaningful to you. Select three or four and commit them to memory. You may find them to be an "iron rod" to you in times of temptation or need. Read again the true experience in chapter 6.

Exercise 10
A Self-Test

Answer the following questions with a yes or no:
1. I read the scriptures at least five days each week.
2. I am regularly involved in a hobby, music, sports, or other activity that I enjoy.
3. I have friends who enjoy life and respect themselves.

4. I have several worthwhile goals for my future that I am actively working toward.
5. I talk to the Lord daily in sincere prayer.

This is obviously not meant to be an accurate or scientific analysis, only to suggest five areas that will help most people avoid problems with immorality. Use it as a guide to improving areas of your life. If you answered yes four or five times you are in better shape to resist evil than one who scored less. If you scored low, you need to be very careful, for you may be more vulnerable to moral problems.

Exercise 11
Once Can Hurt!

Make a list of reasons why you think it is better never to commit a sexual sin than it is to transgress and fully repent later. After you have thought this through on your own, see chapter 4 for some of my ideas.

Exercise 12
Your Own Statement

Review what you have written so far, and then write a summary statement telling why you want to remain morally clean, and *how* you are going to ensure that you do. You might want to read Elder Neal A. Maxwell's eight reasons for remaining morally clean, in his article "The Stern But Sweet Seventh Commandment" (*New Era,* June 1979, p. 43).

As you refer back to what you have written for this chapter, you will find it to be a continual source of strength — of much more value to you than the other chapters of this book. As the months and years go by, add to it, revise it, and you will become firm in your desire and ability to become pure.

Do you remember the Savior's promise to those who are pure in heart? They shall see God! May the Lord guide you as you make

THE CHOICE.

Index

125